Getting a Grip on Your Freshman Year

THE COLLEGE GIRL'S FIRST YEAR ACTION PLAN

Christie Garton

 sourcebooks

Published by Sourcebooks, Inc.
P.O. Box 4410, Naperville, Illinois 60567-4410
(630) 961-3900
Fax: (630) 961-2168
www.sourcebooks.com

Library of Congress Cataloging-in-Publication Data

Garton, Christie.
   U chic's getting a grip on your freshman year : the college girl's first year action plan / Christie Garton.
      p. cm.
   1. College student orientation—United States. 2. Women college students—United States—Life skills guides. 3. College freshmen—United States—Life skills guides. I. Title.
   LB2343.32.G395 2011
   378.1'98—dc22

                                    2010047813

              Printed and bound in the United States of America.
              VP 10 9 8 7 6 5 4 3 2 1

To the women of UniversityChic.com,
the true inspiration behind this book.

contents

· · · · · · · · · · · · ·

college on your own terms

· ·

Congrats! As a freshman in college, you are on a new and exciting path—one that will reflect your own unique interests, passions, and talents. It's pretty exciting when you think about all the possibilities.

Each year there are millions of college students who, like you, are also just getting started, but sadly do not even make it to graduation day. In fact, according to the U.S. Census, one in three students drop out of college for a variety of reasons—bad grades, too much debt, health issues, etc. It's pretty shocking. Of equal concern are those students who do graduate but are unsatisfied with their post-college prospects.

Luckily, there are ways to prevent that from happening to you. The most important thing you can do? Get it right from the start. *U Chic's Getting a Grip on Your Freshman Year: The College Girl's First Year Action Plan* is here to help you do just that. How to use this book? If you've had a chance to check out our bestselling guide to college for women—*U Chic: The College Girl's Guide to Everything*—you'll know that we cover everything you need to know from your first day until you proudly wear your cap and gown. This workbook is an important extension of that guide. Here, we focus on the key building blocks for finding success right from the start of your freshman year, the most crucial time of your college career.

We'll guide you through an action-planning process that has you taking time to figure out what matters most to you and then writing it down. Why is writing things down important? Studies show that journaling your plan for success can actually make the difference between achieving your goals in life or not.

In addition to the action-planning process, we've provided several fun, interactive quizzes and exercises. And of course, as you've come to expect from U Chic, we include tips and personal stories straight from college women who have been there and done it, as well as checklists that pull out the most important points you should take away from each chapter. And when you need more information on a particular topic, you can read the corresponding chapter in *U Chic: The College Girl's Guide to Everything* (noted at the end of each chapter) or head to our website at www.UniversityChic.com. Finally, several sheets of extra paper—"My Notes"— have been provided for you at the end of this guide, for journaling, taking extra notes, doodling, or whatever purpose you choose!

So, that pretty much wraps things up. But before you get started on *U Chic's Getting a Grip on Your Freshman Year*, one last word of advice—have fun with this! Our guide is here to ensure a great first year for you no matter what path you decide to take. So what are we waiting for? Let's get started!

xoxo,

Christie Garton

Founder and Publisher

www.UniversityChic.com

CHAPTER 1

Defining Who You Are

Defining who you are: Sounds like a great idea, right? Unfortunately, not everyone takes the time to do it.

Now that you are finally in college, it is essential to take some time as early as possible to figure out what makes you tick. By figuring this out sooner rather than later, you're better able to take advantage of all those college perks—from study abroad to scholarships to internships—that are uniquely meant for you. Also, before you know it, you will be swept up in so many activities—assignments, deadlines, time with friends, etc.—that you will find it hard to stop, take a deep breath, and think about what you want in the future.

You cannot afford to not give yourself this opportunity to reflect. Your four years in college are essential to laying the groundwork for your future. Once you know who you are, you will have a better understanding of what you want out of life and the goals you need to set to help you get there.

Although it can be challenging, taking the time to define who you are is not only a rewarding but also a fun process! How often do you think about what matters most to *you*?

Consider this guide as your life coach, here to help you figure things out. Let's get started on your path to creating the fabulous college experience on *your* own terms!

WHO ARE YOU, EXACTLY?

I have always been a big believer that who you are is more about what you do than what you say. For instance, I met a young woman recently who just got into law school and is planning to accept. But it wasn't her top choice, and she is a little unsure of whether she is truly meant to practice law.

Hearing these concerns would have normally been enough for me to suggest that maybe she should reconsider her plan for law school. But when I looked at what she *does*—how she spends her free time—I became even more certain that the legal field is *not* right for her. A social media enthusiast, she always seems to be working on marketing projects for friends "for fun." If she considers this work "fun," then she should at least look into how she can make a career out of it before heading to law school. As the saying goes, if you love what you do, you'll never work a day in your life. And wouldn't we all want that!

So let's start by focusing on *what* you do. The best way to start addressing this question is to look back at your past.

Often you didn't have too much of a choice about what you did with your time growing up. Between school, chores, and homework, a good portion of your day was spent doing what others told you to do. But there were occasions when you had complete control over your free time, which is what we are most concerned with here. Think back to these moments of freedom.

When I look back on my past, fifth grade brings back distinct memories of recruiting my friends to create our class's first student-written newspaper. Sure, my compatriots and I may have only managed to get two editions out, but this early experience planted a lifelong fascination with the media industry, which was soon followed in middle school by an illustrated magazine portraying the lives of famous American women throughout history. My teacher had requested a paper. I instantly re-envisioned it as a magazine, which still garnered a top grade despite not having followed the rules.

Looking back, it is no surprise that I have eventually ended up where I am today, publishing an online magazine for women. It was a path that I had set for myself long ago without even recognizing it. That's why I want you to recognize *who you are* today.

How did you spend your free time during these periods of your life?

Grade school/Middle school:

_____

_____

_____

High school:

_____

_____

_____

Now:

_____

_____

_____

See any patterns? If so, note them here:

_____

_____

_____

EVER GET CAUGHT DREAMING?

Now that you've spent some time reminiscing about your favorite activities in the past, take a minute to think about **those dreams** you had long ago, way before all of those extracurriculars, college prep courses, and stressful exams and papers got in the way. Maybe you dreamed of something that you could never see yourself doing today. Florence Griffith-Joyner, a gold medalist in track and field, was my idol in grade school. Unfortunately, my pitiful running skills made sure I would never get close to this idol's significant accomplishments. However, when I analyzed this a bit deeper, I realized Flo-Jo was my idol more for what she represented—strength, confidence, hard work ethic, style (Google Flo-Jo and you'll see what I mean!), and winning attitude—than what she specifically *did*. And sure enough, these are still the qualities I aspire to today.

Take five to ten minutes thinking about your childhood dreams *and* the qualities that these dreams represented for you.

My top three childhood dreams

1. _____
2. _____
3. _____

What each dream represented to me

1. _____
2. _____
3. _____

As you consider your answers in both sections, do you see any connections between the two? Did your activities have any connection to the dreams that you held as a child? For instance, if you dreamed of becoming a famous singer or musician and you spent a significant amount of time practicing an instrument, performing with a music group, or even attending musical performances, you, in a sense, were "on track" to achieving your dreams, perhaps without even realizing it!

But some of you may not have been able to pursue your dreams growing up, due to a lack of financial resources or proximity to training centers and courses in your field of interest. Well, guess what? College *finally* gives you the chance to do what you love! In any case, the key to understanding who you are can often be found in the activities and dreams of your childhood. Once you can define who you are, as you're working to do here, you are well on your way to creating the future you have *always* dreamed about.

Thanks to this little exercise, you are getting closer to understanding who you are and what you want out of life. To sum this exercise up, take five to ten minutes to jot down these dreams that you've honed in on and how you will work to support and nurture them during your time in college:

_____

_____

_____

And if this exercise was not enough, there are additional ways to clarify your interests and passions in life. Many life coaches recommend taking a personality test like the *Myers-Briggs Type Indicator* (MBTI) assessment or participating in Gallup's StrengthsQuest program. These tests can provide more insight into your individual strengths and interests. You can easily find either of these tests by running a search on Google, Bing, or whatever online search tool you prefer.

AND ONE WORD OF CAUTION...

College is not only the place to find yourself; it is also where you'll have a ton of fun. The only problem with that is the fun factor can be a distraction from the most important goals at hand—graduating and, ultimately, finding that perfect job. Our motto for this situation? Work hard; play hard. By finding the right balance between the two, you are guaranteed a great college experience, no matter what.

Anonymous student, Kent State University

You know the most cliché piece of advice you'll ever receive is that college can only be done once, and that you should enjoy it while you can. Now this is a very true rule to live by. But what your parents don't tell you is that you also have to live wisely.

I learned this lesson freshman year, when I decided to get the full college experience. I had spent my first semester cooped up in my room, until finally my friends dragged me out for my first underage drink. That drink turned into many drinks every weekend, throughout the semester. Suddenly I went from prepping for the party to passing out before I made it. My grades dropped, and I have so many nights where I don't remember where I was or who I was with.

If I could do it all over again, I would have asked for more advice. I would have asked how to go against the norm and be who you really are. I am not a huge partier, I have never smoked, and, after a terrible blackout, I now seldom drink. I guess you can say that college is never the same for two different people, but I like that.

Moral of the story? Don't be afraid to go against the social norm and be you, even if that means turning down an underage drink. Your future self will thank you.

FINAL THOUGHTS

Now that you have taken the time to define who you are as an individual, it's time to move forward in figuring out how to make college work for *you*.

CHECKLIST: Defining Who You Are

U Chic's essentials for defining who you are:

- A journal and pen to take notes throughout the book.

- Schedule weekly "me" sessions, taking ten to fifteen minutes to think about the week and how your activities are fitting into your goals for school and beyond.

- Find a mentor who can give you advice on reaching your goals.

- Take additional personal assessment exams like the Myers-Briggs Type Indicator and/or Gallup's StrengthsQuest to better understand *you*.

- Don't forget your passions from the past. These experiences are often keys to a fulfilling (and successful) future.

NEXT STEPS

For more information, go to "Head of the Class" in *U Chic: The College Girl's Guide to Everything* or www.UniversityChic.com.

CHAPTER 2

Class Act

So, what do you want to be when you grow up?

It's a tough question—one that many adults are *still* trying to answer. But that doesn't mean you can't start to figure out your own path now. And the first step in getting on the right path in life is asking yourself this question: "What do I want to achieve in class?"

Do you hope to go to graduate school after college? Or maybe there is a scholarship like the Rhodes, Truman, or Fulbright that you'd like to go after? Or maybe even a fellowship in Congress? If this sounds like you, then you probably know that good grades are essential. For those with less specific goals in mind, no problem. You can still have a general plan of action for the classroom that will have you focused on completing assignments on time or volunteering to lead a class discussion on occasion—each guaranteed to help you get a leg up on the competition.

One quick thing before we get started: We're not here to tell you what these goals should be. That's up to you. What

For those of you who weren't classroom rock stars in high school, no worries. College is your time to shine because now *you* get to decide what you want to study and, ultimately, achieve.

we are going to provide are the tips and tricks for reaching your classroom goals without a hitch.

A Sign of the Times
Ali, University of Missouri

Students are studying less and less, according to University of California Santa Barbara professors Philip Babcock and Mindy Marks. The professors' research shows that the amount of hours a college student hits the books has progressively decreased over the past fifty years.

In 1961 the average student at a four-year institution studied roughly twenty-four hours a week. Students today get in fourteen hours of study time a week. Regardless of the school's size or reputation, or the student's ability level (determined by SAT scores), gender, race, or major, students everywhere are studying less than generations past, according to Babcock and Marks.

Certainly, studying has become more efficient with the advancement of technology. Unlike our parents had to do back in the day, we don't need to search card catalogs for books, get lost in the library on the hunt for elusive texts, or spend hours handwriting notes or pounding out essays on typewriters.

Perhaps students today have more on their plates outside of academia. Many college students have jobs outside of school and participate in a plethora of activities. In this day and age, it's not good enough just to go to class and get good grades; our generation has been told we're capable of great things and that we need to set ourselves apart. Students take on internships, leadership opportunities, and are involved with campus organizations. We're busy! Students may put in fewer hours of textbook highlighting, but that doesn't mean they are any less prepared or educated. Perhaps it's just a sign of our times.

IT TAKES A PLAN

Research has proven that, in addition to using methods that have worked for you in the past, **making a plan and sticking to it** is essential to your success. Consider it your road map for success—one that you can commit to. Your plan will take your end goals and break them down into manageable steps with deadlines.

Here's how it works: Pick any big goal you have. It can even be one you may have for outside the classroom, like that coveted summer internship. Take that end goal—getting an internship offer—and walk backward from that event. Meaning, first you have to **get your resume in order**. Second, you may need to **line up recommendations.** Third comes thinking through your **group of contacts**, and who may already know someone at the company who can get you an interview. And so on. By breaking a huge goal into chunks of more easily achieved sub-goals, you're ensuring an easier path to success in class and in life.

Let's get started by having you create an action plan for success in class that will help you achieve your long-term dreams.

What do you want to achieve?

To get started, answer this question first:

What are your classroom or academic goals?

I can't tell you how I wish someone would have asked me that question at the start of my college career. Sure, I knew that getting good grades was important. My teachers had been drilling that into me since middle school. But I didn't understand the "why?"—Why is getting good grades important to *me*? The understanding of "why" helps ensure that your classroom goals are for *something*. Each action you take. Each paper topic you choose to write. Each relationship you seek to establish with professors. Each of these classroom activities can be geared toward achieving your big goals in the classroom.

"But wait!" you say. "Besides getting good grades, what are some of these other big classroom goals I can go for?"

Collegiate Goals

Here's a short list of potential goals that you might want to aim for in college:

—Graduating with honors or participating in your school's honors program: Many schools give students the opportunity to participate in what is typically referred to as an honors program, which offers top students honors-level courses and seminars, the chance to take graduate-level courses as an undergrad, funding for research projects or travel for national or international conferences, and counseling for national "coveted" scholarships (more about that below). Each school has its own definition of what "graduating with honors" means. Do you need to write a thesis, or is simply participating in your college's honors program or getting good grades enough to meet this goal? If you don't know the answer to this question, then find out by checking with your academic advisor or the department head for your area of studies.

How do you go about getting selected for this program? Your academic performance in high school along with your ACT or SAT score often will result in an automatic acceptance. In other instances, your first-semester academic performance in college can open the door to this opportunity (which is why you're reading about this here).

—Graduating magna cum laude or summa cum laude: I'm sure you've read people's bios with these impressive-sounding words next to their names. Basically what these lovely Latin phrases mean is that someone did very, very well in school and graduated at the top of her class. Dream of having these words follow you the rest of your life? Then you need to start now, planning and working toward this pinnacle of classroom success (more about this later).

—National "coveted" scholarships: If you didn't know it already, there are some fantastic scholarship opportunities for college students that can change one's life. Here are some examples: Rhodes, Truman, Marshall, Fulbright, Barry M. Goldwater, Churchill, Rotary Ambassadorial, etc. Most of these awards provide money for study abroad where a student can further her academic studies. For instance, the Rhodes and Marshall programs provide funding for study in the U.K. The Fulbright and Rotary scholarships provide funding for students in the foreign country of their choosing. Often top grades are one key component of being selected for one of these honors. But more often than not, your specific career goals and related achievements in class are what seal the deal to getting one of these awards. If you can show the awards committee that your specific interests and related classroom success go back to your first year in college, you are putting yourself one step closer to one of these life-changing opportunities. To learn more about any of these awards, your campus most likely has a department dedicated to graduate and fellowship programs for its students (for recruitment purposes, it's in the best interest of the school to have as many of its graduates receiving these honors as possible) and will have someone on staff who can assist you with setting appropriate short-term goals that will put you in the running for one of these coveted scholarships.

—**Study abroad:** Studying abroad has become a rite of passage for many a college student these days. Based on firsthand experience, I can tell you how important this experience can be to your college career. When else in your lifetime will you have the chance to spend a year or semester abroad in a different country and culture, learning to speak a different language and even think differently about the world? Or perhaps your area of study may even informally require an international experience. Either way, this is something you're not going to want to miss. But do be warned that many schools have specific grade requirements before students can even be accepted into a study abroad program. So, be sure to start planning for this opportunity by visiting the study abroad office on campus to learn more about these requirements, and then pursue academic success in the classroom. The result? You are putting yourself one step closer to this ultimate experience of a lifetime, and even more importantly, you can find and secure scholarships that will pay for the experience itself. And of course, for those professions and graduate degree programs (like medicine and law) that require good grades, following this advice is essential. Now that's thinking ahead.

And don't be afraid to ask for advice

These are just a few of the many fantastic opportunities that colleges provide students. Having trouble coming up with something that is important to you? Ask to meet with your academic advisor or your mentor (more on that in a bit), and see if he or she can help identify some goals for you to aim for in college. By starting early in dreaming big and putting in the right amount of effort in the classroom, you're well on your way to achieving any of these goals.

Before we move on, take some time to write down what big goals you'd like to achieve academically in school. Please note we've only provided space for five. If you list too many at the start, you'll never know where to start or how to begin! But don't be afraid to change these or even add to the list down the road as you acquire experience along the way in college that either solidifies these dreams or opens up new paths for exploration.

_____

_____

_____

_____

_____

Breaking it down

Now that you've thought big, it's time to get down to the nitty-gritty—working through the steps to make these dreams happen. For the first step, list all of your goals for the semester and year (no more than three per semester; you don't want to overwhelm yourself at the gate!), and then take several minutes to break those goals down into sub-goals, giving yourself a deadline for achieving each. For instance, a main goal could be "completing one research project and paper in my study area by semester's end," which will take the whole semester to achieve. Next, break that goal into sub-goals that can be achieved in smaller time increments. Here, your sub-goals might include (1) Talking to my academic advisor. Deadline: One week;

(2) Researching potential options. Deadline: End of month; (3) Begin research. Deadline: End of second month. See how that works?

Now, you may not have a clue what you want to achieve beyond the first semester. No worries. Just complete the first semester's goals for now, and then come back later in the year as your ideas start to formulate. Finally, it's always important to pat yourself on the back every now and then. So, as you prepare to knock out your sub-goals, give yourself an extra boost by planning a reward for each accomplishment along the way.

ACTION PLAN: Class Act

First semester
Goal 1: _____

Sub-goal 1: _____

Date for completion: _____

My reward for achieving the goal: _____

Sub-goal 2: _____

Date for completion: _____

My reward for achieving the goal: _____

Sub-goal 3: _____

Date for completion: _____

My reward for achieving the goal: _____

Goal 2: _____

Sub-goal 1: _____

Date for completion: _____

My reward for achieving the goal: _____

Sub-goal 2: _____

Date for completion: _____

My reward for achieving the goal: _____

Sub-goal 3: _____

Date for completion: _____

My reward for achieving the goal: _____

Goal 3: _____

Sub-goal 1: _____

Date for completion: _____

My reward for achieving the goal: _____

Sub-goal 2: _____

Date for completion: _____

My reward for achieving the goal: _____

Sub-goal 3: _____

Date for completion: _____

My reward for achieving the goal: _____

Second semester

Goal 1: _____

Sub-goal 1: _____

Date for completion: _____

My reward for achieving the goal: _____

Sub-goal 2: _____

Date for completion: _____

My reward for achieving the goal: _____

Sub-goal 3: _____

Date for completion: _____

My reward for achieving the goal: _____

Goal 2: _____

Sub-goal 1: _____

Date for completion: _____

My reward for achieving the goal: _____

Sub-goal 2: _____

Date for completion: _____

My reward for achieving the goal: _____

Sub-goal 3: _____

Date for completion: _____

My reward for achieving the goal: _____

Goal 3: _____

Sub-goal 1: _____

Date for completion: _____

My reward for achieving the goal: _____

Sub-goal 2: _____

Date for completion: _____

My reward for achieving the goal: _____

Sub-goal 3: _____

Date for completion: _____

My reward for achieving the goal: _____

Goals I want to accomplish before graduation

Goal 1: _____

Sub-goal 1: _____

Date for completion: _____

My reward for achieving the goal: _____

Sub-goal 2: _____

Date for completion: _____

My reward for achieving the goal: _____

Sub-goal 3: _____

Date for completion: _____

My reward for achieving the goal: _____

Goal 2: _____

Sub-goal 1: _____

Date for completion: _____

My reward for achieving the goal: _____

Sub-goal 2: _____

Date for completion: _____

My reward for achieving the goal: _____

Sub-goal 3: _____

Date for completion: _____

My reward for achieving the goal: _____

Goal 3: _____

Sub-goal 1: _____

Date for completion: _____

My reward for achieving the goal: _____

Sub-goal 2: _____

Date for completion: _____

My reward for achieving the goal: _____

Sub-goal 3: _____

Date for completion: _____

My reward for achieving the goal: _____

Note: If you run out of space above, no problem! We have extra "Class Act" Action Plans for you in the back of the guide.

Now that you've taken the important step of *planning out* your classroom achievements, let's look at some other techniques for ensuring your success.

Find a mentor

One great way to ensure successful completion of your goals? Find a mentor! Why? A good mentor can be an essential part of your success in navigating the choppy and sometimes confusing waters of your freshman year and beyond. Down the road, he or she may end up being a friend and cheerleader for life—something we can all use!

Who should your mentor be? Colleges often assign advisors to their incoming freshmen, which can be a helpful contact for you at the start. Other options include a favorite professor or even a professor with whom you don't currently have a class but who is an expert in the field you want to pursue. Also, don't be afraid to change mentors if your initial choice is not working out for any reason. These individuals are just as busy as you, and will completely understand if your needs are not being met for whatever reason.

How do you line a mentor up? First, you have to do your homework and know who you want to approach. Maybe there is a professor who is doing groundbreaking research in your area of studies. Or perhaps a friend might have a recommendation. Don't be afraid even to ask for other professors' input about who might be the best fit for you.

Once you have someone in mind, your next step is as easy as asking for an initial meeting to get the ball rolling. Don't worry if you have no clue what you want to study in school or even what you're supposed to discuss. Your goal is to get to know them and vice versa.

Once you and your mentor have agreed to work together, you should also aim to establish a monthly meeting time where you can drop in and update them on your progress. And if things don't work out with your mentor for any reason—like a difference in personalities, unrealistic expectations on the part of the mentor, or frequently cancelled appointments—don't let that get you off track! Identify a potential replacement or two, and repeat the same process above.

Mentoring 101

Here are several ways your mentor can help you:

- Identifying goals for your classroom action plan

- Helping you decide which major to pursue

- Planning out the courses you need to take in order to complete your major

- Identifying on-campus resources and scholarship opportunities

- Pointing out potential career paths and internships that fit your academic interests

- Helping with a plan of action if you're struggling with a particular assignment or class

- Keeping you on track

- Being your cheerleader and sounding board whenever needed

So, find a mentor and move forward with your plan for success in class. You'll be glad you did.

Go public with your goals

You've created an action plan and have identified several potential mentors. Or maybe you already have one in place. Don't stop there! There are several other possible members on your support team.

Remember a time when things weren't going the way you'd planned, and you were close to throwing in the towel? What did you do? Did you call a parent or a close friend? Friends and family help provide that extra boost of support right when it's needed or when the going gets tough. Just knowing that they've got your back is enough to keep you focused on the end goal, avoiding the temptation to give up. It's not surprising. As author Wiseman explains in *59 Seconds*, research has proven that once you make your goals public, you are more likely to achieve them. It has to do with you feeling more obligated to complete the goal at hand.

Now that you're in college you have many potential "cheerleaders" to share *and support* your goals. Of course, some of these supporters may be more effective than others. Maybe not all your new friends would be interested in your quest to complete a research project on migratory patterns of birds or obtain an internship in a congresswoman's office on Capitol Hill. But your peer mentor (if your school assigns you one of these), academic advisor or mentor (see above), and even your RA are great potential supporters. Have an older friend pursuing a similar degree or a friend who has achieved a similar goal? Don't hesitate to ask them for their input. If you've hit it off with your roommate, don't be afraid to reach out to her as well. You see each other every day, so what better person to help keep you inspired (and you the same) toward reaching your goals? You can even team up with a friend to help keep you both on track toward achieving your goals. All of these individuals care about your success in school, so don't hesitate to reach out.

Time to review

Before we move ahead, let's take a quick moment to review. To achieve success in the classroom, whatever your goal may be:

1. Make a plan;

2. Go public with it; and

3. Don't forget to take a break and reward yourself for your hard efforts.

Just roll with it

This step-by-step approach to classroom success all sounds simple to do, right? Maybe not. What happens if the problem is just getting started, meaning you know *what* to do each step of the way, but the main problem you're having is the lack of spark or ignition to get the ball rolling.

As with many problems in life, the solution here may be simpler than you expected. In the case of procrastination, where something is blocking you from starting a project for class, just get moving. This means that the best thing you can do is just begin working even if you don't feel 100 percent ready to do so. Wiseman in *59 Seconds* calls this the "just a few minutes" rule. There is research out there that shows just spending a few minutes getting started with a project makes it more likely that you will feel an "urge to see it through to completion."

Why is this technique so effective? Basically, by getting started with a project, term paper, or presentation, the few minutes of initial activity cause your brain to refuse to rest until the job is finished. It's simply a biological reaction! Bottom line: if you're having trouble getting started with a project, my best advice is to just get started with it and your brain will help move you along.

But what if something else is holding you back from even getting started? Stress is often the silent culprit. Here's an exercise to see how you handle stress along with some essential advice for putting a lock on it.

POP QUIZ: How Do You Handle Stress?

Stress can be a great motivator, but it can also be debilitating and impede your success if you're not careful. Do you work well under pressure, or do you cave when the stakes get too high? Take this quiz to determine you overall stress quotient.

1. **Your homework assignments are piling up and your sorority sisters or dorm mates are bugging you to chair the spring formal. How do you handle it?**

   A. Say no and focus all your energy on your class workload.

   B. Tell them you need a week to plow through your homework and once you have a handle on it, you'll get back to them on your availability.

   C. Give in to their guilt trip and spend the next month barely sleeping because you're so busy.

2. You're assigned a group project for class, but no one but you seems motivated to get started. What's your plan of attack?

A. Just focus on your part of the project and hope the rest of your group manages to get their work done before deadline.

B. Organize a group meeting and create an action plan.

C. Do the whole project yourself.

3. Your dorm room is disgusting, but the only time you have to clean is during the big championship game on Saturday afternoon. What's your solution?

A. Pick up what you can and hope you find your chemistry book before Monday's test.

B. Pow-wow with your roommate and agree to set aside a half an hour each day to clear the clutter.

C. Ignore all the dirty dishes and piles of clothes and just go to the game.

4. Disaster! A semester's worth of history notes just got trashed when your roommate tripped and spilled her entire glass of water all over your book bag. What's your first reaction?

A. Scream at her and then scramble to find a way to salvage them.

B. Do your best to maintain composure as you go through your class contact list and try to locate someone close by who will let you borrow theirs.

C. Burst into tears and stomp out of the room.

5. You've been pulling a ton of all-nighters before midterms and you wake up with a fever and sore throat the day of the exam. The best thing you can possibly do is:

A. Drag yourself out of bed and beg your boyfriend to drive you to the campus clinic ASAP.

B. Email your professor, explain the situation, and let him or her decide if you can do a makeup.

C. Pop some aspirin and hope you can make it through class without passing out.

Mostly As: Your response to stress is reactionary rather than proactive. Stop waiting for things to get bad—if you think ahead and plan accordingly, you can divert a lot of these issues before they become a major problem.

Mostly Bs: You're pretty well-balanced when it comes to obvious stressors in your life and seem to have a knack for not allowing yourself to get all worked up over things that are out of your control.

Mostly Cs: Stress? What stress? You spend so much time avoiding it you've managed to create a snowball effect. If you nip things in the bud early on, many of the problems you face will most likely disappear.

Don't forget to deal with the hurdles

As with all challenges in life, even with the best plan in mind you will eventually face some hurdles. A few of these obstacles may be higher than others. But if you put in a little up-front effort to deal with these potential potholes, you'll be well on your way to seeing your goals through to the end.

What do we mean about putting in a little up-front effort? Simple. Go back to your plan that you started above and add a new entry to each: "Potential Hurdles." Here is some space for you to add these:

Goal 1/Potential Hurdles: _____

_____

Goal 2/Potential Hurdles: _____

_____

Goal 3/Potential Hurdles: _____

_____

Goal 4/Potential Hurdles: _____

_____

Goal 5/Potential Hurdles: _____

_____

Try to envision what types of hurdles might present themselves during the journey to your end goal. Next, list ways to minimize their impact or, better yet, how to completely avoid them. By arming yourself with a strategy for dealing with these roadblocks, even if it is bare bones to begin with, you will already have the mind-set that you can deal with any hurdles, and they *won't prevent* you from reaching the end zone.

Since your potential hurdles are unique to you, we won't spend too much time focusing on what may arise. However, there is one hurdle that affects so many of us, it's worth briefly addressing here. I'm talking about past failures—ones that inhibit us, preventing future success.

We've all had failures—those times when we did not achieve our desired outcome. And in all cases of failure, we have two possible choices for next steps: We can either let it be a lesson that can help us to future success, or we can let it be a stumbling block, in the form of fear of more failure.

Knowing your options, which would you choose? The former, right? But when you're in the heat of the moment of a recent failure, it is hard to take a step back and see the big picture. But you have to; you owe it to yourself. To help get you there, never forget this point: College is the ultimate testing ground with four years of exploration at your disposal, which includes succeeding and, yes, occasionally failing at things. If you already had it all figured out, why did you decide to go to college, anyway?

MANAGING TIME LIKE A PRO

We couldn't possibly move on without addressing the all-important topic of time management (which we'll refer to here as TM). If there is one thing that will guarantee success in school, it's the ability to successfully manage your time. Study too much, you won't have time for fun, but study too little, and you're likely to fail.

Before we dive into how to manage your time like a pro, let's take a minute to explore your current TM skills.

POP QUIZ: How Are Your Time Management Skills?

Do you have a knack for keeping everything straight, or are you already feeling stressed and falling behind? Answer these questions as honestly as possible.

1. How many times a week do you find yourself running late for class?

   A.   Pretty much *every* day.

   B.   Maybe once or twice depending on the workload.

   C.   Hardly ever.

2. It's Monday, and you just found out you have an essay due Friday. When do you start it?

   A.   The night before. You'll usually pull an all-nighter and then get it done with minutes to spare.

   B.   Midweek. It's tight, but it's still enough padding for you to do research and double-check your work.

   C.   On Monday. Why put it off when you know you have a ton of other things going on?

3. Your typical night involves the following:

   A.   Work out, grab dinner, spend an hour texting with your boyfriend, gossip with your roommate, and THEN start your homework.

   B.   Grab something to eat, go through your to-do list, and then simultaneously work on your homework in between cleaning your room or doing a few loads of laundry.

   C.   Retype your notes, finish your homework, organize your work space, and *then* go look for something to eat.

4. The weekend is fast approaching, and you've inadvertently double booked yourself for your BFF's b-day back home *and* a date with the hot guy two floors down from you. How do you rectify the situation?

A. Rush home Friday night, spend time with your BFF, speed back Saturday evening, stay out all night, crash Sunday morning, then scramble to get your homework done while nursing a hangover.

B. Convince both of them that it's easier if you all hang out together and plan a big Saturday night out near campus.

C. Lie to your BFF and tell her you have a test to study for and just hope she never finds out you ditched her to go on a date.

5. Your friends usually complain about the fact that you:

A. Are always late and completely scatterbrained.

B. Try to take on too much sometimes.

C. Put way too much pressure on yourself.

Mostly As: Disorganization and procrastination are ruling your life, and it's obvious to everyone but you that you're in danger of crashing and burning. Take a step back and look at the big picture. Exactly what do you gain from putting off everything? Instead of ignoring stress, *own it* and create a workable schedule that allows you time to still do the things you enjoy.

Mostly Bs: You're pretty good with hitting your deadlines, but you could be better. Stop trying to be everything and just be YOU. It's OK to pass up a party invite or bail on your study group once in a while. You can't be an expert multitasker if you're constantly running on empty.

Mostly Cs: You've got this multitasking down pat, but be careful that you're not throwing your life out of balance. Yes, getting good grades in college is important, but so is having fun with your friends, eating healthy, and giving your mind and body time to rest and recoup.

So how did you do? Could your TM skills use a little brushing up? Being able to juggle multiple tasks while keeping your head above water is the single most important thing you can learn in college.

Facebook and Your Grades

There's just no way around it: Facebook is a fact of life these days. Nearly 90 percent of college students have a Facebook account. However, recent studies have found that Facebook may not be the best way to spend your free time in school. Indeed, college students who use Facebook spend less time studying and have lower grade point averages than students who have not signed up for the social networking website, according to a pilot study at one university. Although 75 percent of Facebook users say that the social networking site didn't interfere with their studies, their grades seemed to show otherwise. Indeed, Facebook users in the study had GPAs between 3.0 and 3.5, while non-users had GPAs between 3.5 and 4.0. This could have something to do with the amount of time they spent on Facebook when they could have been studying, as users said they averaged one to five hours a week studying, while non-users studied eleven to fifteen hours per week.

As we'll say here and throughout the rest of the book, we're not here to tell you that you shouldn't use Facebook. In fact, Facebook—as you'll read later—can be very beneficial in getting and staying connected on campus. We're just here to provide the facts to help you make the best and most informed decision for yourself. And in this case, you may want to think twice before killing numerous hours on Facebook in place of studying.

Here's some very good advice I came across in Kate White's *Why Good Girls Don't Get Ahead but Gutsy Girls Do*. White, editor-in-chief of *Cosmopolitan*, writes that a "gutsy girl" (that's you!) should only do what's essential, which pretty much boils down to doing only that which helps you reach your goals in life. Basically, don't overextend yourself.

How does this apply to your work in the classroom? Go back to your action plan. Something that can get in your way of these goals may be the tendency to want to overdo it, White explains. During your first semester, you may be a bit nervous and tend to take too many credit hours, study too hard, and generally go overboard. How to avoid this tendency? Focus on your essentials—the goals set out in your action plan—and the mini-steps that go into each one. If an extra class or the Saturday review sessions you're planning aren't going to make an appreciable difference in helping reach your semester goals, then forget about it.

The work-hard-play-hard attitude will do you well in college. Plan to work hard when you're studying, but when you're not, enjoy the moment because you *need* these fun and relaxing times as well. This balance between work and fun will keep you in top form to the end.

GETTING MOTIVATED

Chasing your goals requires effort and, more importantly, motivation. But if you're like most of us, the tendency to procrastinate can sometimes get in the way. Are there tricks for getting and staying motivated? Definitely. But before we take a look at some of these proven techniques, let's consider what doesn't work.

In a new environment with no mom or dad telling you when to study or go to bed, it is common to throw routine to the wind in favor of late nights out with friends and too few hours in the library. But to find success in the classroom, you have to avoid this temptation. You have to get and stay motivated.

Think first about what strategies got you moving in the past because, most likely, they're still going to work for you in college. Which methods worked? What did your high school teachers or sports coaches use to help you get motivated in the classroom or on the field? Take a moment to list them here:

_____

_____

_____

Which of these techniques might work well for you in college? Did some work only because you had someone enforcing a study period? Maybe you were an incessant planner and were always writing down your to-dos for the next day. Keep doing that! And don't be afraid to take one of these tactics and tweak it to fit your new collegiate life.

One Study Technique to Avoid

When applicable, academic shortcuts are great, but only if they work. Here is one technique you may want to reconsider. Did any of your coaches or teachers ever have you try a visualization technique—one that asks you to close your eyes and imagine yourself achieving that end goal? Visualization techniques have long been a popular tool used by the self-help industry for achieving one's long-term goals. Unfortunately, there is overwhelming evidence that, although they may make you feel more confident about the goal, these techniques are largely ineffective.

In Richard Wiseman's book *59 Seconds: Think A Little, Change A Lot*, one featured study had a group of students daydream or visualize getting a high grade on a midterm exam while another group, the control group in the study, continued with "business as usual" and did not daydream. The result? The students who imagined themselves receiving a big fat "A" on the exam actually studied less and received lower grades than the group who did not daydream at all. Other studies have found that daydreaming or visualizing that job or internship promotion or even getting a date with your crush will not lead you to success. Moral of these studies? Visualizing your goals may make you feel more confident, but nothing works better than cracking open the books.

One Study Technique to Consider

While daydreaming might not help you reach your goals in the classroom, psychologists at the University of Chicago have discovered a quick and easy way for stressed-out students to avoid choking on high-stakes tests: Take a few minutes right before the exam to write about all those fears.

According to a recently published study in *Science*, anxious students who were given ten minutes to put their feelings down on paper performed significantly better than their peers who wrote about other topics or did nothing at all.

So what does this mean for you? If you find yourself anxious before quizzes or exams, try writing about these feelings in a journal right before the test for ten minutes, but no longer. The study's authors caution against spending too much time dwelling on negative thoughts. This simple task—when given the right amount of time—may lead you to better test scores in the end.

BUT I WANT TO HAVE FUN, TOO!

"But wait!" you say. "College isn't all about studying." We completely agree. If you work the time management skills we walked you through above, you'll have more than enough time to play. And that's something we could all use a little more of! If you're still on the fence on whether time management skills are even worth the bother, read the following personal story from one of UniversityChic.com's bloggers as a precautionary tale:

Blair, University of Miami

By the end of my freshman year I was in full-on party mode. My first semester had been stressful; it took me awhile to find a good group of friends and really adjust to my new surroundings. When spring rolled around, I not only had friends but also a semester's worth of built-up party energy. I continued to work hard at my classes, but they weren't really classes that demanded too much time or attention. There was plenty of time to lounge around in the sun (going to college in Miami has its perks) and spend time with my newfound friends. Of course, since I was a good student, I also did the reading for my classes and did all of the necessary assignments. I made sure not to procrastinate or save too much for the last minute.

This ended up being the key to my finals success. Although I had been in school for almost a year, I was still a freshman, and still not convinced that doing karaoke until 4:00 a.m. the night before a Mexican history final was a bad idea. Thankfully, I woke up with about an hour or so to spare before heading to my test, and since I had done all of my homework and studying in advance, my fun night didn't hurt my grade (I got an A!). Moral of the story? Work hard, and playing hard won't hurt you.

If you need some extra help in finding balance and staying focused, plan to make a weekly schedule each Sunday, listing out all of your to-dos. A great way to do this is to use a student planner like our *U Chic College Planner*. Most planners include a monthly calendar and weekly break-out section that allows you to plan those long-term goals discussed in this chapter. You can use the weekly section to plan out your activities that are helping work towards the sub-goals you listed in the "Class Act" Action Plan, ultimately helping you meet those long-term ones. By sticking to your action plan, using a schedule, and building in time for fun, you're ensuring a smooth and successful ride all the way to the end.

FINAL THOUGHTS

Do you think you have what it takes to achieve your goals in the classroom? Now that you're equipped with the essential advice you need and an action plan for success, you are well on your way to being one class act in school and in life.

CHECKLIST: Class Act

U Chic's essentials for getting and staying ahead in the classroom:

- Breakfast. Have a protein-based meal in the morning to get you revved and ready to succeed.

- Good night's rest. No explanation needed, right?

- Start with a plan. With your action plan driving your classroom efforts, you're guaranteed to succeed.

- Post-class review. And review, review, review again!

- Find a study buddy and build a "support team" that can provide the extra boost to keep you on track.

NEXT STEPS

A lot of the advice provided so far (i.e., finding a mentor and going public with your goals) applies to the goals you will set throughout the rest of this book. For more information, go to "Head of the Class" in *U Chic: The College Girl's Guide to Everything* or www.UniversityChic.com.

CHAPTER 3

Campus & Community Maven

We spent the last chapter talking about what it takes to be successful in the classroom. However—as you've probably heard—in college it's not always about what happens *inside* the classroom but *outside* class that can matter the most. By becoming an involved campus and community maven— someone who knows the ins and outs of life outside of the classroom—you are ensuring a fabulous college experience and life after college.

YOUR NEW HOME

Before diving into the exciting world of college extracurriculars, you need to first get to know your new home. As a first-year student in college, you may experience a bit of homesickness. But guess what? Most students miss home at first—it's a rite of passage, as U Chic writer, Tracy, explains:

Tracy, Binghamton University

Moving in to your college dorm for the first time is a piece of cake (a sometimes emotional piece of cake, but cake nonetheless). When I went into my building for the first time, my RA immediately greeted me with a big hug and showed me to my room. With the help of my older sister, unpacking only took two hours and before the sun set, I was waving my sister goodbye.

Settling in is the simple part. What comes afterward…not as simple.

Homesickness is a strange thing. You spend so much time anticipating freedom while living under your parents' roof, and then suddenly, all you want is that old familiarity and structure college life may lack. My biggest issue was that I really missed my pets. I wasn't used to walking into my room and not having my dog tackle me at the door. At one point, I even closed my eyes and hugged a random dog someone on campus was walking—just because it was about the same size as my dog.

There are no tips or tricks when dealing with homesickness. All I can say is that like any other kind of heartache, it passes with time. Even if they eventually seem to bleed into one another, home will always be home, and school will always be school. The best advice I can give? Don't make your dorm room a mock-up of your room at home. You're in a completely new environment, so embrace it!

Whether you're homesick or not, one of the best ways to come to love your new home is to get out and see it. So in this spirit, here is a fun exercise for you—a college scavenger hunt! (NOTE: If you're reading this as part of a class, make sure your classroom instructor follows the only rule for the hunt: the class should meet *outside* the classroom for this scavenger hunt to be a success.)

EXERCISE: College Scavenger Hunt

Think you know everything about your school? Put your knowledge to the test! Grab your camera and a notepad, and let the hunt begin! Partner up with someone and locate the following items at your school. The first group to complete the task (make sure you take pictures as proof) wins! (We'll leave the prize up to you or your instructor to determine.)

- The oldest statue or monument on your campus

- Most popular spot for weddings and engagement proposals

- The last winning pennant or trophy your school received

- Campus Security Office

- The closest emergency call box/pay phone

- Where students go when they're feeling under the weather

- Student activities office: The place where students go to learn about on-campus activities and clubs

We hope you had a blast with the scavenger hunt. If, for whatever reason, you're not able to get out with a class to see the campus, gather a group of friends and challenge them to a hunt or get yourself out of the dorm room, as U Chic writer Olga did when she arrived at college in Boston:

Olga, Boston University

I got lucky living in Boston, where I was surrounded by history, culture, and one of the best college towns there is. Visiting other colleges gave me a chance to meet people from everywhere and to escape my own university when I needed to. Also, Boston's rich culture and history allowed me to visit one of the oldest taverns in the U.S. and visit old Italian eateries in the North End. The new weather (new for me—a Californian) was the perfect way to get to know the city as well, because I got to go ice skating, go pea coat shopping, and discover just how great hot chocolate tastes on a cold winter day. The first snow was always an amazing day for me! I made it special!

THE CAMPUS DOWNLOAD

So now that you know your campus better, it's time to start thinking about how you want to be involved in school. If you haven't discovered it already, you will soon find out that a lot of class time is dedicated to theory. However, as important as this theory is to your life in the classroom, it's not always going to come in handy after college when you're having real-world challenges, like troubles with the boss or first-time client meetings. The best way to prepare for the real world after college? Get involved on campus and in your community where you can get as close as possible to real-world experiences.

But wait. Before grabbing a list of possible activities and joining every group that sounds cool, it's important to be strategic about your options. You need to think about which activity is the right one for you based on your *own set of personal goals in life*. Translation: Don't be the student who gets involved just to be involved. Before you know it, you'll be swamped with meetings to attend but hardly any meaningful experiences to show.

As you did for the classroom, you also need a plan for life outside of class. Here is an exercise to get you started:

POP QUIZ: Which Organization or Activity Is Right for You?

Getting involved is a great way to network and make new friends. Not sure where your interests truly lie? Take this quick quiz to determine your group style.

1. **When you get together with your friends, you're usually:**

   A. Meeting up in between classes or on the weekends to work out, run, or do some fun outdoor activity.

   B. Organizing some big group outing or coordinating some fun event like a party, concert, or trip to the mall.

   C. Obsessing over your favorite TV show/new album/latest movie.

   D. Launching new projects, whether it was a tree house or lemonade stand as a kid or recruiting friends for a charitable activity like a run or walk now.

2. **What kind of role do you take on when in a group of friends or classmates?**

   A.   Teammate—you're an active participant, but you don't try to run the show.

   B.   Taskmaster—you like to keep everyone on track.

   C.   TV commentator—you're up-to-date on all the latest news, gossip, and dorm room dramas.

   D.   Leader—you're the leader of the pack, whether it means campaigning for student body president votes or deciding plans for Friday night.

3. **Be honest: How dedicated are you when you're involved with something you like?**

   A.   Daily. When you make a commitment to something, you stick with it.

   B.   Weekly. School comes first and everything else is a close second.

   C.   Monthly. Your life is too crazy to try to schedule anything else on a regular basis.

   D.   Always. You build your interests into everything you do.

4. **What's your favorite part of being involved with a group?**

   A.   Feeling like you're part of something important.

   B.   Building connections and long-lasting relationships.

   C.   Just chatting and getting to know people with similar interests.

   D.   Making things happen.

5. **What teams or groups were your favorites in high school?**

   A.   Sports and theater

   B.   Student government

   C.   Clubs and extracurriculars

   D.   All of the above

Mostly As: You're dedicated, determined, and would make the perfect teammate for any of your college's sports programs. Make it a point to go to some events and see which one is right for you.

Mostly Bs: Talk about the ultimate sorority sister! Look into rush opportunities at your school and take time to chat up some of the sisters who may live in your dorm.

Mostly Cs: Short on time but big on enthusiasm? Research unique campus or community activities that appeal to your personal interests. It's a great way to meet new people and bond over your shared obsessions.

Mostly Ds: You were born to lead. Find an activity or group that allows you to put your natural skill for leadership to work, like student government or being the president of your favorite organization on campus. Haven't found the right activity for you? Start your own! For all you born leaders, there is nothing more fun or gratifying than building your organization from the ground up.

What did you learn? Is student government your thing? Or maybe you have an idea for a new group on campus. Stop by the student activity office on campus to check out different organizations, or look them up on the web. For possible off-campus opportunities, consider joining a church in your neighborhood, getting involved in local government, or volunteering for a local nonprofit. (Often your student activities office will have this information as well.) Either way, you now have some great thoughts on what activity is right for you, so it's time to start with a plan of action.

WHAT'S OUT THERE?

Let's get started with an action plan for how you're going to make your dreams in life happen by getting involved outside of class.

ACTION PLAN: Campus & Community Maven

To create your action plan for outside of class, start by choosing your top three goals in life. Don't stress too much about what they are right now. Just follow what your heart tells you. Reference the list of activities on campus and in the community, and then pick the ones that seem to be most related to your goals, along with the level of involvement that you'll need to commit to making them happen.

I've filled out a sample one to help get you started:

Sample goal: Running for public office

Possible activities: Student government; volunteering for local nonprofit; local school board

Level of involvement: Run for a leadership position for any of these organizations

Goal 1: _____

Possible activities: _____

_____

Level of involvement: _____

_____

Goal 2: _____

Possible activities: _____

_____

Level of involvement: _____

_____

Goal 3: _____

Possible activities: _____

_____

Level of involvement: _____

_____

Note: If you run out of space above, no problem! We have extra "Campus & Community Maven" Action Plans for you in the back of the guide.

Not sure if some of these activities are relevant to your goals? Test them out by going to a few initial meetings to see whether they seem like a good fit and are something you might become passionate about. If after attending a few sessions you're not thinking it's a good match, drop the activity as soon as possible. College is too short to waste any time on activities that are not right for you. By being strategic about your time outside of the classroom, you are taking one giant step toward achieving your goals in college and in life.

Facebooking Maven

As you read earlier, Facebook has been linked to lower grades, but can it affect your relationships? While the study found that Facebook users had lower grades than non-Facebook users, students who were more involved in extracurricular activities at school were more likely to use Facebook. There's a good reason for this. Facebook is a fantastic way for you to quickly connect with others of similar interests and find resources for getting involved on campus and in the community.

But proceed with caution here as well. Just make sure that you don't spend all your time socializing online rather than off. A good rule of thumb: For every hour you spend on Facebook or other social networking sites, plan to spend at least the same amount of non-Internet hours getting out, involved, and familiar with your new home and the movers and shakers on campus.

FINAL THOUGHTS

Are you ready to hit campus running now that you have a plan of action? We think you are. Last piece of advice? Have fun, but also be safe.

CHECKLIST: Campus & Community Maven

U Chic's essentials for getting involved:

- Familiarize yourself with the campus and community first.

- Be strategic about your options. Don't join every club just so you can say you're involved.

- Don't be afraid to test out the waters, so to speak. Try out as many activities as you think you might be interested in, just make sure to drop the ones that aren't important to you.

- Invite your new friends and roommate(s) to join you. Getting involved together is a great way to build friendships and experiences that will last you a lifetime.

- For every hour you spend on Facebook or other social networking sites, plan to spend at least the same amount of non-Internet hours getting out, involved, and familiar with your new home and the movers and shakers on campus.

NEXT STEPS

For more information, head to "Getting Involved" in *U Chic: The College Girl's Guide to Everything* or www.UniversityChic.com.

CHAPTER 4

Sorority Life

With college comes many choices. One of the biggest decisions you can make is whether joining a sorority is right for you.

Forget what you've seen in the movies—sororities aren't all about boys, parties, and mean girls making you feel bad about yourself. They're about sisterhood, community, and forging a bond that will last well beyond your college years (as evidenced by the fact that the first sorority was formed over 150 years ago!).

The importance of this special bond can be traced back to the origin of the word "sorority" itself. The Latin root "soror" means "sister" in the English language, further establishing the importance sororities place on the support and development of their members, academic success, and setting a high standard for both moral and community excellence across the board.

In today's world, the typical sorority girl is neither blond nor rich—she is everyone and everything. She comes from a varied background, is smart, outgoing, and has an interest in supporting charitable and environmental causes that are near and dear to her heart. Sure, she likes to have fun, but making a difference and getting good grades ranks at the top of her list.

Sororities 101

Wondering if the other things you've heard about sororities are true? Here's a quick primer:

Fact: Sororities DO have standards, but they have little to do with looking like a supermodel and wearing designer duds.

These rules and regulations usually include moral and academic behavior, like getting above a certain GPA and not doing anything that could tarnish the chapter's reputation on campus (i.e., cheating on a test, having crazy parties, and destroying public or private property).

Fiction: You have to be really rich to be in a sorority.

While finances do play a role in being an active member (after all, you are expected to pay your semester dues), most sororities offer payment plans and financing for members in need.

Fact: Joining the sisterhood is almost like having a full-time job.

There's no such thing as part-time membership! When you're active in a sorority you're *active*—as in attending weekly meetings, planning events, doing charity work, etc. If you're not ready to commit that much of your time to one thing, sorority life probably isn't for you.

Fiction: Sorority girls are really cliquey and only hang out with their own sisters.

OK, there's no denying friendly rivalries between sororities exist, but that doesn't stop most girls from seeking friendships outside their comfort zones. While it's only natural that your bond with your sisters might be stronger (after all, you *do* spend quite a lot of time together), nobody is going to look down on you if you have a separate circle of friends who aren't into Greek life.

YOUR SORORITY ASSESSMENT

If you're ready to give some serious thought to joining a sorority but aren't sure where to begin, it's a good idea to consider your motivation first before you throw yourself into the process. Take time to answer the following questions as honestly as possible (we've provided space to write your answers or you can just think through them as you go!):

What do you already know about the sororities on your campus?

_____

_____

_____

_____

How do you perceive each one from an outsider's perspective?

_____

_____

_____

_____

What are your reasons for wanting to join a sorority?

_____

_____

_____

_____

Have you taken time to weigh the pros and cons of being a full-time member?

_____

_____

_____

_____

What unique traits or skills do *you* bring to the table? (After all, it's not just about what makes a sorority great—it's what makes *you* a standout!)

_____

_____

_____

_____

Review your answers and use this as a starting point. Once you have a basis for why sorority life might be right for you, you can then move forward in figuring out which chapter on campus is right for you.

GETTING STARTED

"Rush," or officially "membership recruitment," is a lot like going on a job interview—research, rehearsal, and presentation are key. You are the "potential new member" (or PNM), and they are your potential new sisters.

The average recruitment cycle contains four rounds that slowly whittle down the crowds to the individuals each sorority is interested in recruiting. These rounds include open house, skits, philanthropy, and final preference. The process wraps up with a "Bid Day" where each sorority extends a certain number of invitations to the women who they hope will join their house. But wait; it's not over yet! If you choose to accept one of these invitations, you are not automatically a member. Instead, you will have to go through an initiation period of several weeks (more on that below). Here's the bottom line on the recruitment process and what to expect:

- *First Round—Open House*: This round is when you, the PNM, get to visit all of the sorority houses on campus. This is an informal opportunity to meet women from all of the sororities; it can sometimes take two days if there are a large number of sororities on the campus. At the end of the round, you, the PNM, get to select a number of sororities you would like to visit again. The sororities also select the PNMs they would like to visit their homes again. The Panhellenic Council (Panhel) brings all of the information together and generates a list of invitations for each PNM for the next round. Feel free to wear jeans, but make sure you look your best!

- *Second Round—Skits*: The second round usually features skits that each sorority prepares to show the PNMs what life is like at their chapter. After you visit all of the sororities to which you were invited back, you again narrow down the list to your favorite ones. The sororities also narrow down their list of their favorite PNMs. Panhel once again tabulates the information and generates the invitation lists for the next round.

- *Third Round—Philanthropy*: Whew! You're almost done. Each sorority has a national philanthropy in which it actively participates. During the third round, you will spend time doing something related to the sorority's cause. It usually involves crafts or making something and is a casual activity. It is also a great time to get to know more of the sisters in each house while talking informally. Once this is complete, you will go through another round of narrowing down your list to your favorites, and the sororities will do the same. Panhel tabulates the information, generating an invitation to the last round of recruitment.

- *Fourth Round—Preference*: Now that you've visited all of the houses and have narrowed down your list, you're ready for the fourth and final round— "preference." This is a more formal, ceremonial round, and everyone will be dressed up. It usually involves a ritual-like ceremony that speaks more meaningfully about the sorority, sisterhood, and the sorority's symbols. After attending all of the Preference parties, the PNMs and sororities once again must make their decisions. The mutual selection process ends when Panhel matches the PNMs and sororities according to the lists provided by each. But you're not done yet!

- *Bid Day*: The day has arrived when you find out which sorority has selected you! Typically, the PNMs will all gather in one location and receive an envelope that includes the name of the sorority to which they've been matched. Once you open your bid and know the results, you are then dismissed to find your new sisters. Afterward, you will participate in a pledging ceremony, followed by an initiation period where you will be educated in the history and background of the group and integrated into the sorority. During this period, you will most likely become very close to members of your pledge class as you work through the steps toward becoming an initiated member of the house.

Sororities Doing Good

If you think being a sorority woman is just about partying, you've got it all wrong. Sororities were established to encourage academic excellence, friendship, and more importantly, giving back to the community.

Philanthropy, both in terms of donating money to charity and spending time volunteering, is a virtue upon which each and every sorority prides itself. Each national sorority has a philanthropic cause that all its chapters work to help. Each collegiate chapter then creates its own philanthropic event to raise money (like a campus basketball tournament, a charity kickball game, or a male beauty pageant).

Check out this list to learn the national philanthropies of each National Panhellenic Conference sorority:

Alpha Chi Omega: Domestic violence awareness and The MacDowell Colony

Alpha Delta Pi: Ronald McDonald House Charities

Alpha Epsilon Phi: The Elizabeth Glaser Pediatric AIDS Foundation and Sharsheret: Linking young Jewish women in their fight against breast cancer

Alpha Gamma Delta: Diabetes awareness and education

Alpha Omicron Pi: Arthritis Foundation and the American Juvenile Arthritis Organization (AJAO)

Alpha Phi: Women's heart health and research

Alpha Sigma Alpha: Special Olympics and the S. June Smith Center

Alpha Sigma Tau: Pine Mountain Settlement School and Habitat for Humanity

Alpha Xi Delta: Autism Speaks

Chi Omega: Make-A-Wish Foundation

Delta Delta Delta: St. Jude Children's Research Hospital

Delta Gamma: Service for Sight

Delta Phi Epsilon: Cystic Fibrosis Foundation, Anorexia Nervosa and Associated Disorders, and the Delta Phi Epsilon Educational Foundation

Delta Zeta: Speech and Hearing and the Painted Turtle Camp

Gamma Phi Beta: Camp Fire USA, Girl Guides of Canada, and the Gamma Phi Beta Foundation

Kappa Alpha Theta: CASA (Court Appointed Special Advocates)

Kappa Delta: Girl Scouts of the USA, Prevent Child Abuse America, Children's Hospital in Richmond, Virginia, and the American Academy of Orthopaedic Surgeons—Orthopaedic Research Awards

Kappa Kappa Gamma: Reading is Fundamental (RIF)

Phi Mu: Children's Miracle Network

Phi Sigma Sigma: National Kidney Foundation and the Twin Ideals Fund

Pi Beta Phi: Literacy initiatives and First Book

Sigma Delta Tau: Prevent Child Abuse America, Jewish Women International, and Women for Women International

Sigma Kappa: Gerontology, Alzheimer's disease, and Inherit the Earth

Sigma Sigma Sigma: Hospital "play therapy" programs

Theta Phi Alpha: Glenmary Home Missioners and the House That Theta Phi Alpha Built

Zeta Tau Alpha: Breast cancer education and awareness

And here is the list of national philanthropies associated with National Pan-Hellenic Council's historically African American sororities:

Alpha Kappa Alpha: Global Leadership through Timeless Service

Delta Sigma Theta: Delta Research and Educational Foundation

Sigma Gamma Rho: Habitat for Humanity, Operation Big Book Bag

Zeta Phi Beta: Z-HOPE (Zetas Helping Other People Excel)

Certainly, recruitment can be stressful and challenging at times. However, most participants feel that the effort is well worth the time and expense to enjoy the benefits of a lifelong sisterhood. And of course if, along the way, you decide that it's not right for you, that's completely OK too!

POP QUIZ: Which Sorority Is Right for You?

Still not sure which sorority on campus is a good fit for you? Why not try narrowing down your choices based on some of the traits that best define your current interests and lifestyle? Take this quiz and then use it as a guideline when you meet with chapters during rush week.

1. In your free time, you usually like to:

   A.   Volunteer or organize charitable drives for your dorm.

   B.   Spend time studying and catching up on your class reading.

   C.   Relax and spend time with your friends.

2. When it comes to going out with your friends, you're usually the one who takes on which task?

   A.   All the planning and preparation.

   B.   Mapping out where you're going and checking it out online.

   C.   Doing whatever is asked of you but not stressing about the details.

3. When you're at a party or event, you're usually the one who's:

   A.   Rushing around helping the host or hostess pick up trash and refill plates and glasses.

   B.   Monitoring how much everyone is drinking to ensure no one drives home drunk.

   C.   Playing social butterfly.

4. Which of these three things ranks highest on your priority list?

   A.   Staying involved in what's happening on campus and joining new groups to better prepare yourself for a job in the future.

   B.   Getting good grades and keeping your GPA up.

   C.   Networking and making connections.

5. What do you hope to get out of being in a sorority?

   A.   Lots of experience, plus great contacts in the future.

B.   To learn more and gain valuable insights about yourself.

C.   To make friends and expand your social circle.

Mostly As: You're the gal with a plan, super-organized, and have energy to burn—what part of that *doesn't* scream "charity-focused sorority"? Given your great organizational skills and need to be involved, you're exactly the type of person who could do community outreach, put together an event, or spearhead a major online campaign to get your entire campus involved in some philanthropic project.

Mostly Bs: Learning. Studying. Excelling. You may not be an education major, but you have that inquisitive and nurturing spirit that makes you the perfect candidate for an academically-driven sorority. Just imagine yourself tutoring your sisters, or even creating an after-school mentoring program for underprivileged kids. It's these kinds of skills that make you a standout, so don't be afraid to talk up all that you've accomplished.

Mostly Cs: You're not much for strict rules and you could totally do without a regimented schedule that requires you to spend hours and hours planning and plotting some big shindig or charity fund-raiser. If you're not ready to commit yourself full time to a big national sorority, a local chapter may be more your speed. This way, you get the best of both worlds: the community and spirit of being part of the sisterhood without the hindrances of having to rearrange your life to accommodate previously established guidelines and scheduled events.

GETTING PREPARED

Before you even sign up to go through recruitment, you absolutely *have* to do your research. You wouldn't walk into a job interview unprepared, right? Recruitment is no different. Sororities are looking for potential members who are engaged in the process, know what each chapter is all about, understand the responsibility that comes with being a sister, and can answer each of the above questions (not to mention why you're the perfect fit!) with grace and candor.

Resources

A good place to start is with the National Panhellenic Conference website (www.npcwomen.org). The NPC represents twenty-six national sororities around the country and provides links and information regarding history, tenants, founding members, charitable alliances, etc. First identify which sororities are active on your campus, then set out to learn more about each one because not all sororities or chapters are alike. For instance, the Alpha Gamma Deltas at one school may be politically inclined with several members in student government while the Alpha Gams at another may be more into sports with several college athletes as members. Do you share the same goals and values as the Pi Beta Phi girls? Are you into the idea that Kappa Kappa Gammas place a high priority on academics? Does the fact that the Chi Omegas are actively involved with the Make-A-Wish Foundation gel with your own charitable interests? To better understand these differences, visit each sorority's national headquarters website in addition to any locally based version that may exist.

Slowly but surely, you'll start to get a really good sense of which chapters match your personality and individual style. That's not to say you shouldn't explore the other ones (after all, that *is* a huge part of the actual rush process), but this should help you form an overall opinion once you get a chance to meet and chat with the active sorority sisters and hear what they have to say about it.

Know your sorority lingo

If you want to walk the walk, you gotta talk the talk. Sororities and fraternities have special words they use to describe people, places, and events that define important aspects of Greek life. Ready to school yourself on all things sorority? Make sure you add these terms or phrases to your vocabulary:

Bid: An exclusive invitation given to individuals who are asked to join the sorority.

Executive Board: Commonly referred to as both the E-Board or Leader's Council. Typically, this board often includes a sorority or fraternity's president, vice president, rush and social chairs, etc.

Greeks: The name given to members of sororities and fraternities, which they use to identify themselves by combinations of Greek letters.

Initiation: A special event or ceremony for new pledges that officially kicks off their membership in the sorority.

Legacy: A Potential New Member who is closely related to a woman with membership in a National Panhellenic member sorority. The definition of a legacy varies from sorority to sorority, but it almost always includes a woman whose mother, sister, aunt, or grandmother was a member of a particular sorority. Legacies are usually given special consideration for membership, but sororities are not required to invite them to membership.

Mutual Selection: The process during membership recruitment when the sorority members seek the women who will best enhance their sisterhood and the Potential New Members determine which sorority will be the best fit for them.

Panhellenic Council: The governing body that controls all sororities and fraternities on campus. Panhellenic officers make all the rules and take action when a sorority or fraternity steps out of line. Members are often executive officers from the many Greek organizations that reside at a specific college or university.

Pinned: New sorority members are given a pin to wear that designates them as a member of the sorority. Typically, you receive this pin during an official ceremony.

Pledge: New members who have accepted their bids but have not yet been initiated into the sorority.

Pretty Playbook: The rules or guidelines on what to wear during rush. Usually sororities will hand out fliers or post instructions on their websites or Facebook pages to help guide you on what's appropriate for each event.

Quota: The number of women a sorority can offer a bid to during recruitment. This number is determined by the Panhellenic Council.

Recruitment Counselor (RC or Rho Chi): Formerly known as Rush Counselors, these are sorority women who disaffiliate with their own chapter during recruitment in order to help the Potential New Members with the selection process. They offer impartial support and answer questions during membership recruitment.

Recruitment Week: Also known as "rush week." This is when potential members attend parties and meet the sisters of each sorority.

Rushee or Potential New Member: A term used to designate potential members.

Socials: These are also known as mixers, socials, or themed parties held by various Greek chapters.

ACTION PLAN: Sorority Life

Now you have an idea what to expect when rushing and know the lingo for the process. Ready to move forward in exploring sorority membership? It's now time for you to create a plan of action.

As we previously discussed, meeting potential sorority sisters is a lot like interviewing, so it's important to have something to offer to the conversation that shows that you're invested in the success of the sorority itself. Here's a simple step-by-step process for getting ready to rush.

STEP 1: Familiarize yourself with the sororities on campus and what makes them tick.

Having this knowledge in your back pocket will not only impress your potential future sisters, it will also give you something to fall back on if you run out of things to say.

What were some of their recent events on campus? What was the impact?

What charity fund-raisers did they hold?

Were there any great accomplishments by certain members? (i.e., Was a member selected as a top Greek member on campus?)

Did the chapter receive campus or national awards for its efforts?

STEP 2: Think about ways your background and experience can aid each sorority in its future success.

One way to help you stand out from the crowd of other PNMs is to offer up ideas on how *you* can make a difference within each chapter. This is great practice for when you have a *real* job interview, plus it helps you to better define the special characteristics and traits that make you a stand-out. Come up with a list of five skills or qualifications you can use to differentiate yourself from your fellow rush participants. Here's a list of questions to get you thinking:

Are you an amazing planner?

A whiz with technology?

Do you get really good grades, and are you open to tutoring other sisters?

Do you have a talent for singing or stage performance that could come in handy for the annual spring talent revue?

STEP 3: Create a list of talking points.

Every college freshman who's taken Psych 101 knows that we're all drawn to the familiar. In laymen's terms, this means we subconsciously want to be around people and places that are in sync with our own likes and beliefs. This is why talking points unrelated to sorority life can be extremely helpful.

Obsessed with *Twilight*? Love to bargain shop? Concerned about the environmental impact the oil spill in the Gulf Coast will have on wildlife ten years down the road? Write up a list of five to ten topics that you can use as conversation starters. These subjects are *exactly* what you will need to gain inroads with potential sorority sisters and new friends you might meet along the way during the rush process.

List them here:

1. _____

2. _____

3. _____

4. _____

5. _____

6. _____

7. _____

8. _____

9. _____

10. _____

Note: If you run out of space above, no problem! We have extra "Sorority Life" Action Plans for you in the back of the guide.

Got your plan of action ready? We now want to focus on one of the most essential items in the recruitment process—the art of conversation. Most likely, you will not know any of the women you'll be meeting during the sorority recruitment process. If you're truly invested in joining a sorority, the best way to make it happen is to make yourself seen and heard (but not in an obnoxious way, of course!).

Don't be afraid to go up to someone and introduce yourself during a rush event. You might be surprised to discover one little conversation starter could eventually lead to the bid of your choice!

Here are some examples:

What made you want to join XYZ sorority?

What do you think separates your sorority from the others on campus?

Can you tell me a little bit about some of the events you've worked on recently?

Which fraternities are you affiliated with?

What words would you use to describe your chapter?

What characteristics do you look for in potential pledges?

What projects or initiatives are you looking to expand on in the near future?

These are great ways to break the ice, and could put you in the lead for a spot in the house of your dreams.

Before we wrap up, let's take a minute to address some of the common questions and concerns that can come up when pursuing sorority life.

QUESTION: What should I wear during recruitment?

ANSWER: Wear what makes you feel comfortable and confident. You want to put your best foot forward during the process, and you can't do that if you're worried your boobs might pop out of that tight dress.

Here are some other dos and don'ts on dressing for recruitment:

Do make it memorable: The sorority members will meet dozens and dozens of women, and it can be a challenge keeping everyone straight. Make an impression by wearing something memorable—though not obnoxious!—so that the sorority members will remember you when it comes to choosing who they want to invite back.

Do keep it classy: At all costs, avoid showing too much boob, booty, or leg. You do *not* want to be remembered as the hoochie mamma that came through.

Don't wear something trendy just because.

Do get a mani/pedi/wax ahead of time.

Don't spend extra money on an outfit unless absolutely necessary; and you definitely do *not* need designer duds in order to secure a bid.

Do break out a nice pair of jeans, sundress, and cocktail attire.

Still not sure what to wear? Here's some great advice straight from U Chic's Pretty Playbook.

Your Pretty Playbook (What to Wear When Rushing)
Kristy, University of Illinois at Urbana-Champaign

Rush is vastly different depending on what school you go to, where you attend, and how large of a Greek system exists on your campus. While there is no universal hard-and-fast rule as to what you should wear, here are some general guidelines on how to look your prettiest without giving off the wrong impression.

1. You're rushing a sorority.

I know what you're thinking. "Duh. That's why I'm reading this section." But honestly, I can't emphasize this enough—you're not going to a frat party, or a club, or even looking to snag a hot guy. There's no need to show off a ton of cleavage or wear a short skirt that makes your butt look amazing. Just remember, you're trying to impress girls with style—not the male ego. Think pretty, *not* sexy. Also, the little details *do* count. Guys don't care about manis, pedis, or if you bothered to get your eyebrows waxed this week. But we of the opposite sex do notice those sorts of things, so make sure you're primped, plucked, and presentable before you sign up.

2. Yes, there are levels of fashion formality to follow.

Again, this changes depending on which school you go to, but typically rush starts out more casual and gets more formal as the events progress. When I rushed (and this seems fairly standard for the most part), there was an event where jeans or shorts were worn and T-shirts were provided. The first invite is typically slightly less formal, so opt for a nice skirt and sandals. Second invites usually require casual sundresses, while the third invite is typically the most dressy (cocktail-type numbers might be required).

3. Trust us, money isn't everything.

If you're in love with your oh-so-expensive True Religion jeans and feel the need to wear them for rush, go for it. If you feel more confident and comfortable in your favorite pair of Levi 501's, that's totally fine too. Choose what you think best represents your style and personality—not the most expensive item in your wardrobe. This obviously doesn't mean that you can just show up wearing an old pair of sweats and a T-shirt (again, these are girls, and frankly, we live in a world where style and fashion *do* matter), but, overall, if you really get along and connect with a house, it shouldn't matter if you're sporting Bebe or Betsy Johnson.

4. Accessorize, accessorize, accessorize!

The members who are rushing you (i.e., the active sisters of the sorority chapter whom you'll be meeting and chatting with) see a ton (like *hundreds*) of girls each day. Outfits start to blend together, and in a time when retail stores are everywhere, not everyone can have an original ensemble. That's why it's absolutely *critical* to accessorize with pieces to highlight your unique look and show off your personality and style. Plus, if someone ends up wearing the same dress or fancy top, you'll still be able to rock your outfit without feeling one ounce of insecurity. Warning: Don't plan on accessorizing with purses or clutches. These are typically left outside during rush, and some schools even provide everyone with large identical tote bags to decrease the possibility of someone's expensive purse getting jacked by a frat boy (true story—it's happened).

5. Choose clothes that make you look and feel good.

So much of what goes into being chic isn't about having the "right" pair of jeans or even the cutest dress—it's about wearing something that makes you look your best. Don't try to squeeze into a size 2 skirt if a size 4 or 6 actually fits you better. Just pick out something that makes you feel good about yourself. That alone should make other people want to know where you got all that confidence (and style!).

QUESTION: If, after doing the research and taking the quiz, I'm still not sure that sorority membership is right for me, what should I do?

ANSWER: The absolute best way to find out if sorority life is right for you is to go through recruitment. You are by no means expected to join a house if you do—it's a time to discover what you want to do. The other benefit of going through the process? You are certain to make new friends along the way, helping you transition into college life, sometimes more quickly than those who don't rush.

QUESTION: How much does it cost to join a sorority?

ANSWER: While being in a sorority is one of the greatest experiences college has to offer, it can also be very costly if you're a student on a fixed budget, or if you're attempting to pay for it all on your own without the help of your parents. Most likely, you'll find that making a timely investment in the sisterhood extends to monetary costs you might not have even considered.

Sorority Expenses: A Breakdown
Kelly, San Francisco State University

Initiation and Dues

The largest fees you will pay when joining a sorority are your initiation fee and your dues. You may be asked to pay each one separately or in a lump sum (that's what my sorority does). In my case, all new members are required to pay an annual due of $1,200, but for returning "active" members, it only costs $800. This works as an incentive to discourage members from dropping out or going inactive for a year. Keep in mind that payment plans can vary greatly, from every two weeks, to monthly, per semester, or annually. Some sororities like mine will also work with you to come up with a personal payment plan if any of these don't work with your budget. Obviously this is something you should research before you commit yourself and find you're forced to live on water and ramen noodles.

Sorority "Extras"

Most sororities are "all inclusive." This means that if you attend an official event, your dues will likely cover all your expenses. But keep in mind that dues don't include a lot of things that are considered unspoken "extras" or necessary evils. It won't cover your date's tickets for events, or the new outfit you will want to buy. It also doesn't cover any gift exchange that you do, or unofficial outings with the girls, like going to the movies or out to dinner. The amount you spend on these things ultimately depends on how involved you want to be. Plan on spending an extra $30 to $70 for scheduled calendar events, and make sure you put aside $20 to $30 a week for "socializing" time with your sisters.

Dressing Like a Sister

Many times, your sorority will want you to dress in uniform. They will provide you with house letters and any T-shirts that are needed, but there are also some basic items that you will need to purchase in anticipation of other events, like rush (such as denim skirts, or a certain color high heel). No, you won't need a new outfit for *every* major party or social, but you will need to stock up on a lot of basics to ensure you meet mandatory dress code requirements.

Housing

Think your dorm is expensive? The cost of living in your sorority's house can often be double that of your initial initiation fee per semester. Typically, second-year sisters and the sorority's executive board all live under one roof in an official Greek residence, or off-campus depending on local ordinances and housing availability. On the flip side, it can be even *more* expensive to find housing on your own if your school is located near a major city like New York, Chicago, Boston, or San Francisco. Once you factor in $1,300 to $1,700 per month for an apartment, furniture, utilities, and food, paying a lump sum of $6,000 to $8,000 a year (meals included) seems pretty reasonable by comparison.

Like any investment in life, joining a sorority can appear financially daunting when looking at the overall big picture. Again, while cost can play a major factor in your choice, be realistic about what you hope to gain from becoming a sister. If you're looking to immerse yourself in the entire experience, then paying a little extra shouldn't be a big deal. If you're looking for a fun way to meet new people and socialize? Well, don't feel bad if other options like becoming active in your dorm, joining a school club, or taking up a team sport fit more into your financial framework.

For me, joining a sorority was a no-brainer, but you should definitely weigh the pros and cons carefully before you commit yourself to something you ultimately might not be able to afford.

QUESTION: What happens if I go through the entire process of recruitment and don't receive a bid?

ANSWER: There are many reasons why someone may not receive a bid at the end of the process, including:

- Not meeting a sorority's minimum GPA requirements
- Immaturity/poor self-image
- Inability to attend recruitment events due to involvement in other activities

- Poor judicial standing with the college or university

- Showing a lack of interest in the chapter

- Not treating chapter members politely or with respect

- Not completing the formal recruitment process

Some of these potential issues can be circumvented with preparation. Unfortunately, others cannot. If it happens to you, for whatever reason, you should not feel embarrassed or bad about the outcome. There are plenty of other fulfilling options for you to get involved on campus, and you should not spend a minute longer dwelling on this. Move onward and upward, as we like to say!

Here are some other options for you to consider:

—Informal or open recruitment: Often after formal recruitment, some chapters will still have open spots and can extend bids. Also, some sororities may "snap bid" the women they want and will not announce that they are still recruiting new members. Other sororities will hold informal recruitment activities in the following days or weeks in order to meet potential new members, even those who didn't go through formal recruitment. We also want to point out that not all sororities will participate in open recruitment, as they've already met their quotas, leaving you with fewer chapters from which to choose. But for women who want to join a sorority and are willing to be open-minded about their options, open and informal recruitment can provide an opportunity to still join a sorority that year.

—Try again: If you did not receive a bid, you can choose to wait another year and try again at the next formal recruitment. This can work well for women who had a low high school GPA that hurt them with sororities that had to cut based on higher GPA requirements. If you get better grades your freshman year, you will greatly increase your chances of joining a sorority.

An added bonus from waiting another year: You get the opportunity to network on campus, potentially meeting and making friends with current sorority members. This can be an asset when going through recruitment next year, as being known (in a good way, of course!) can make a potential new member more attractive to the sorority members.

One word of caution: If the sororities on your campus are known for extending bids primarily to freshmen, being a sophomore can make it almost impossible to get a bid. As this varies widely from campus to campus, it's important to do your research and know what the options are for rushing as a sophomore or junior.

—**Start a new sorority on campus:** Didn't get a bid but still want to be part of a sorority? Avoid going through the process by starting your own! But as you can imagine, starting a sorority is a lot of work and takes a tremendous amount of time and commitment. Also, there are no guarantees it will be a success or that the group will be able to eventually affiliate with a national group. But it is always an option and one to consider if you're a natural born leader.

Classroom Assignment: Create Your Own Sorority

Sometimes you don't get a bid. Other times, you find that the sorority you've chosen just isn't a good fit. Whichever the case, that doesn't necessarily mean you're not cut out for Greek life.

More and more, students across the country are founding their own local sororities to fill gaps they see on their campus. Sometimes these sororities are based on race, religion, or educational background; others simply grow out of students' need to feel like they're a part of something without the typical costs and constraints usually associated with a national chapter.

In an effort to better understand how a sorority works, you're tasked with creating a proposal that demonstrates why a particular type of sorority is necessary for your school. Research the current Greek chapters at your institution, look at the demographics of students on campus, examine the average household income, and then develop a presentation to support your argument. Make sure you answer the following questions as you progress through this assignment:

1. Which would be better: a brand-new local sorority or a chapter for a preexisting one not already on campus?

2. How many members could you possibly reach with your unique scope?

3. What would differentiate your sorority from the others at your school?

4. Would you have your own house? A meeting place? How would this impact membership dues?

5. Which local or national charities would you target? What kind of events would you host? How would these two things tie into your overall message or scope?

Once everyone has completed their proposals, nominate members of your class to act as your "Panhellenic Council." Members will then cast their votes on the most innovative and thoughtful plans and then offer their feedback.

—**Embrace the independent life:** While there are benefits to sorority membership, there are also many other ways to be involved on campus, as you read about earlier in this book. Thus, another option is to be a proud and happy independent.

Although failing to receive a bid from a favorite sorority can feel like the ultimate rejection, we can guarantee that if you talk with anyone who didn't receive a bid, they'll tell you that it was the best thing that could have happened. And as they say, things always happen for a reason.

Do you think you've got a handle on this thing called sorority life? We think so. No matter what you end up deciding to do, we wish you all the best with your decision. It's going to be great!

FINAL THOUGHTS

Thinking about joining a sorority? Treat it like a job or internship interview. Do your homework, come prepared, and let your confident self shine through! Here's a checklist to get you started:

CHECKLIST: Sorority Life

U Chic's essentials for deciding if a sorority is right for you:

- Know what makes you special and what contributions you could bring to a chapter. This is great information to provide potential sisters when going through the recruitment process.

- Do you have friends going through recruitment with you? It's great to share your experiences and rely on each other for support, but don't let their opinions or choices sway you on the decision you think is best for *you*. After all, this is *your* fabulous college life.

- Put all stereotypes you've ever heard about the sorority experience behind. By going into the process with an open mind, you're putting yourself one giant step closer to finding out what's right for you, no matter what happens.

- Did you go through the process but didn't get a bid? Don't let this outcome get you down. You have plenty of options for what you can do next. The goal is to *move on* and don't look back.

NEXT STEPS

For more information, head to "Sorority Chic" in *U Chic: The College Girl's Guide to Everything* or www.UniversityChic.com.

CHAPTER 5

Relationships

I n college, you're dealing with a variety of relationships—professors, roommates, coworkers, new friends, significant others, etc. These relationships are important to your success in school and beyond. In fact, according to several studies, to have a "thriving" or successful day, we need six hours of social time, which includes everything from hanging with friends at school, work, on the telephone, and even by email.* Sure it's common sense, but who knew that socializing with others is scientifically proven to help you thrive? In this chapter, we're going to look at the most important types of relationships you'll have in college, in order to help you be your best. Before we get started, U Chic writer Olga has some good advice on transitioning from high school to college, from a relationship perspective:

Olga, Boston University

Starting anew in college gives you a clean slate, with high school far behind you. It is a chance to reinvent yourself and, though it may be hard to make friends at first, literally try everything. Nobody knows who you are, so invite strangers to come with you to events you hear about. Chat up the people sitting next to you in class about what they are doing this weekend. Hang out with anyone and everyone because you will never get the chance to have this clean slate again.

ROOMIES: FRIENDS OR FOES?

First week orientation. New classes. New schedule. New home. New faces. When you're just getting started in college, everything is new, which can certainly be overwhelming at first.

One important relationship that you'll be dealing with during that time is the one with your new roommate, a person whom you've likely just met for the first time—unless you decided to room with a friend from high school (though that can present its own set of unique challenges).

We can't stress it enough—a good relationship with your roommate is key to surviving and thriving your first year in college. But note that we're not saying that you have to become best friends with your roommate. If you do, that's great. But what we're talking about is establishing a healthy, working relationship—one where there's an open line of communication that goes both directions.

Don't like the fact that her high school sweetie is coming for a visit and shacking in your tiny dorm room every other weekend? Can't stand it that she's IM-ing friends until the wee hours of the morning while you're trying to sleep? Maybe she feels that your general messiness is cramping her style? Either way it goes, each should feel comfortable enough to tell the other how she feels. Otherwise, you both will be spending too much precious time being stressed about the entire situation, and that's not conducive to a fabulous college experience.

So, how does one go about building a successful relationship with a roommate?

> Get to know your roommate from the very start. Don't wait until the beginning of second semester.

What are some ways to do that? During the first week, invite her to get out of the dorm to grab a coffee or ice cream. We can't stress the part about getting out of the dorm enough. Here are some other great techniques for you to consider:

Be proactive and reach out to your roommate(s) as soon as you get your room assignment. Think of this like a job interview. You should be asking them all about their likes and dislikes ahead of time so you can get a better sense of who and what they're all about.

Set ground rules right when you move in. Don't wait until a problem comes up—address it well before the school year gets under way so that you're both on the same page. Make it clear what your deal breakers are (overnight guests, messy living space, etc.) and then come up with a reasonable compromise.

Bring a welcome gift on the first day. Create a positive first note for your relationship by beginning it with a thoughtful gift that shows that you're invested in getting to know your roommate better. Try a plate of your mom's homemade cookies or a unique gift from your home state that says "Hello! Can't wait to start living together!"

Make a concerted effort to leave your drama at the door. Don't make your roommate your favorite punching bag. If you're stressed or unhappy about school, use him or her as a sounding board—*not* an easy excuse for someone to scream or yell at.

Use a mediator when things get tense. If you find you and your roommate can't meet somewhere in the middle, don't just leave things as is. Instead seek out your RA or dorm advisor to act as a mediator. An outside perspective might be able to offer you an unbiased opinion or solution to the problem.

Still wondering how to make the most of the situation with your roomie(s)? Read how one student built a successful relationship from the start:

Victoria, Quinnipiac University

I think of New Haven as my second home, and a lot of that had to do with having a successful relationship with my roommates. How did I go about building those relationships? Well, I love getting to go to different restaurants and local hangouts and tried to include my roommates in that fun as much as possible. Through it, we've been exposed to a variety of new things—for example, my first year I decided to go out to an Ethiopian place and it was amazing!! I've been back almost every semester and always have an urge to try new foods. Experiencing new foods also helps create a bond with your roommates.

By getting out of the dorm like Victoria did, you're leaving behind the complicated dynamics of dorm living during the first several weeks. That way, you have the peace and quiet to really get to know a potential new friend and ally who can help make the transition to college that much easier.

Before moving on, it's worth taking stock of your current efforts as a roommate just in case there may be room for improvement that you weren't aware of.

POP QUIZ: Are You a Good Roommate?

Navigating the new roomie waters with minimal drama can be a challenge. Test your coping/compromising skill with this quick quiz.

1. Your new roommate is all hearts and flowers when it comes to decorating, while you're big city cool and love modern touches. What's your plan of attack?

A.   Sit down with her and try to find some common ground. You're willing to can the whole black-on-black theme if she gets rid of her Jonas Brothers posters.

B.   Agree to decorate each side of the room in your own style and keep the bathroom as is.

C.   Complain to her that you just spent the last four years in the same room as your little sis, and there's no *way* you're doing the Hello Kitty thing again.

2. For the past few weeks, you and your boyfriend have been crashing in your room, since his is beyond messy. You can tell it's been bothering your roommate, so you:

A.   Schedule a time to discuss it with her. Better to clear the air than get the silent treatment.

B.   Designate official "together" time with your boyfriend each week and give her the head's up in advance when he'll be over.

C.   Ignore her. It's not like she doesn't have her friends from home visiting *every* weekend.

3. **You have a big exam, you've been studying all night, and you missed dinner. The only food in the room happens to be hers and you're *starving*. It only takes a split second for you to decide to:**

A.   Drop her a quick text asking her if it's OK if you snag something from her snack drawer.

B.   Dig in, but leave her a note that you'll restock her stuff tomorrow.

C.   Help yourself without any guilt. It's not like she's going to care, right?

4. **The hot RA your roommate has a crush on invites you to go to the big game on Friday with him and all his friends. You think he's cute, but...**

A.   It's not worth the drama. You'd rather pass and save yourself the big fight that's sure to follow once she finds out.

B.   You can't say yes until you talk to her and feel out how deep her feelings are.

C.   You swear him to secrecy and make him promise not to tell your roommate the two of you are hanging out.

5. **OK, so you totally love your roommate, but your BFF just found a *dirt cheap* apartment off-campus for next semester. You want to take it, but you already agreed to room with your roommate for another year. You tell her:**

A.   The truth. Honesty is the best policy and you hope she understands.

B.   You'll help her find a single on-campus so she doesn't have to totally stress during finals.

C.   Right after you sign the lease. You guys are cool, but it's not like she's your best friend or anything.

Mostly As: You work off a "separate but equal" mentality, which is fair most of the time but doesn't always leave room for empathy. Just because you're living on your own doesn't mean you're *all alone*, so try to take her feelings into consideration more often.

Mostly Bs: You're the queen of compromise. Often it's *you* who finds a working solution you both can agree on. This is a great attitude and will serve you well later in life when you're forced to balance the needs of many against your own.

Mostly Cs: OK, she's your roommate, and not your sister. Mom isn't around to come along and intervene when the two of you get into a fight. Now is a good time to accept the fact that you're an adult who is responsible for the relationships you're building—positive or not.

With this advice on how to have a good relationship with your roomie(s) now in your back pocket, you might just have a great BFF or supporter waiting behind your dorm room door.

A CURE FOR THE HOMESICK BLUES

Have you been on campus for several weeks—long enough to get past the normal period for homesickness—and are still dealing with the homesick blues? It's time to take action.

Take a moment to assess what you've been doing so far to ease the transition. What activities have you been up to? List them here:

_____

_____

_____

_____

_____

Notice any trends? Are you spending too much time studying in the library? Eating out by yourself? Going home on the weekends? Several of these strategies are typical tactics that homesick individuals take to avoid feeling homesick. But when you consider it, none of those activities do anything to help you actively deal with those nagging feelings of homesickness. You can do more to get to know the new people around you. Choose activities that get you out and meeting people on campus.

There are two things you can do to make dealing with homesickness easier: leave your door open, and turn your phone off. Of course, if you're about to head out to the shower, feel free to close the door for some privacy. But if you want to make new friends in your dorm, the best way to do that is to send the signal that you're friendly and you're there to hang out. It's much easier to meet new people when your door is open and they can hear your music playing or see your dorm decorations. It gives them a reason to stop in and say hello.

Leaving your phone off is probably the more difficult of the two things, but it may also be the most helpful. If you need your phone to meet up with new college friends, then don't totally abandon it. But at the very least, give yourself a week or two before you allow yourself to call your high school friends, or maybe even your parents. Once you get past the initial point of needing to talk to them because you are homesick or lonely, you'll probably already be much more comfortable in your college setting and will only need to call them to catch up or talk about your weird professor, not complain about how much you miss home.

Kick That Homesickness to the Curb!

Here are some additional homesick blues-busting activities to try:

- Get involved on campus. Follow your action plan from chapter 3, and start getting out and getting to know people who have similar interests as you.

- Plan to eat many breakfasts, lunches, and dinners at your dorm. Most importantly, don't be afraid to sit with a group you've never met.

- Plan to hang out in the commons area of your dorm several times a week—it's a fantastic (and cheap) way to meet a lot of people fast.

- Sign up to lead or participate in as many dorm activities or events as possible.

- Sorority recruitment. Even if you do not plan to join a sorority, the sorority recruitment process is a fantastic way to get to know a ton of people who will remain friends, whether you join a house or not.

Trying new activities, and establishing a routine with more social time built in, will cure your homesickness before you even know it, as it did for Olga:

Olga, Boston University

The best thing about freshman year is that we did everything and anything. I hung out with a different crowd every weekend, and it gave me a chance to see where I fit in in this new college world. In addition to different friends from classes, groups, and my swim team, I found different places to be.

One weekend I was at a frat party, and the next I tried a college-organized roller hockey event. One weekend, I went to see a band play at a local venue with a friend from class, and the next weekend I visited a posh Ivy League party in a cocktail dress with a friend from high school. Nothing is lame unless you decide it is…so it's best to just give it all a chance.

Before we move on, take a moment to write down your plan for tackling any homesickness you may currently be facing. By making a plan, you're taking one giant step toward conquering these common feelings that many college students face the first several weeks in school.

ACTION PLAN: Relationships

What are some new ways you can try to conquer that homesickness? We've filled out an example to get you started:

Goal: End homesickness

1. New Activity: Sign up for intramural basketball.
    How Often: Practice twice per week.

2. New Activity: Audition for the school choir.
    How Often: Practice once per week.

3. New Activity: Go through informal sorority recruitment.
    How Often: Can start as soon as I contact the Panhellenic Council office on campus.

Now it's your turn. Try to come up with at least three new social activities to try:

Goal: _____

1. New Activity:_____
    How Often:_____

2. New Activity:_____
    How Often:_____

3. New Activity:_____
    How Often:_____

Note: If you run out of space above, no problem! We have extra "Relationships" Action Plans for you in the back of the guide.

We should note that if—after several weeks of engaging in these new activities—you're still feeling down, you may have a more serious problem than pure homesickness. If so, there are plenty of on-campus resources that can help you deal with these feelings. Do not hesitate to seek help from an RA or at your on-campus health center.

DATING IN COLLEGE

And of course we couldn't talk about relationships without addressing the all-important issue of dating in college or dealing with the opposite sex.

To start off, here's a fun quiz to determine how well you handle living and loving in a mixed environment.

POP QUIZ: Can You Read between the Lines?

College is full of new life experiences, and one of the biggest challenges is adapting to an environment where everything isn't always spelled out for you. Take this quiz to determine if you're on the same wavelength with that certain "someone" down the hall…

1. **Your secret lab crush asks you over to his room to cram for a test. This obviously means:**

   A.   Um, he wants you to come over and study with him (duh).

   B.   He's secretly into you, too!

   C.   It remains to be seen. If his room is totally nice and neat when you get there, the feeling might be mutual.

2. **The guys two floors down are having a huge weekend bash, but for some reason you're pretty much the only person in the building who hasn't gotten an invite. What's the deal?**

   A.   You're not sure, but you're going to make it a point to sorta hang out in their hallway later and see what happens when you run into them.

   B.   They totally hate you.

   C.   Most likely they told someone to invite you and that person flaked and forgot.

3. **You and your significant other got into a huge fight and now he is totally MIA. Worst-case scenario?**

 A. He is probably out doing something stupid with his friends.

 B. He's hooking up with someone else!

 C. Please. The big baby is most likely hiding out in his room pouting.

4. **You have this professor who constantly runs you down and calls on you in class. Either he's out to get you, or:**

 A. He's not a morning person.

 B. He just hates you.

 C. He's trying to use some lame reverse psychology method to get you to work harder.

5. **Uh-oh. Your BFF is dating this girl, but she has been rather sketchy about where she lives. What's your theory?**

 A. She lives with her parents.

 B. She's probably a messy person and embarrassed about it.

 C. Sounds like someone's got a roommate by the name of Girlfriend.

Mostly As: OK, so you're no expert on reading people, but you have a pretty good idea how most tick. Don't jump to conclusions and never make assumptions. Sometimes actions *do* speak louder than words.

Mostly Bs: Reality check: Sometimes it's not all about you. It's easy to think the worst when you don't have all the facts. Practice better communication techniques and simply ask if you're unsure. You might be surprised to learn that most people are more worried about *your* perception of them than vice versa.

Mostly Cs: Could we have a budding psychologist in our midst? You've got a knack for understanding people and seem to grasp that outside variables and past experiences can sometimes color our perceptions of situations. Keep up the good work and try to be the voice of reason when one of your friends automatically assumes the worst.

The Changing Face of Hook-Up Culture on Campus
Kylie, Harvard University

My mom is pretty cool, all things considered. She texts, she has a Gmail account, and she even knows the difference between an iPhone and an iPad. Unfortunately, the definition of this term "hooking up" remains elusive to her, often resulting in hilariously awkward conversations that start something like, "Oh honey, since you're working in New York this summer, maybe you and Jane Morris's son can hook up one evening for dinner." Or, "Honey, here's Benjamin's phone number—you go to school in the same place and I've been waiting for you two to hook up forever!"

I understand my mom is from a different generation in which courtship and serious dating were the norm, so I can see why she might be a little confused. But how to explain to my own friends, who seem a wee bit hazy on the definition as well?

Some refer to a dance floor make-out as a hook-up. Others say hooking up is an appropriate term to describe any action up to third base, while still others refer to it as the whole (naked) nine yards. Despite the various definitions swirling around out there, the main implication of a statement like "I hooked up last night" is uncommitted, sexual action with a friend, acquaintance, or stranger.

The fact that the phrase "hooking up" has become such a common term says something about today's teens and young adults. The changing culture of college dating and sexual relationships has dramatically altered the way women view their own sexuality. While the sexual revolution in the 1950s and '60s brought the advent of the birth control pill and Women's Lib, the twenty-first century has ushered in a whole new crop of coeds who have casually declared their bodies open for business.

And guess who's listening? Believe it or not, some college campuses have sex toy workshops, erotica weekend conferences, and full-blown sex weeks (even in the formerly stuffy Ivy League—here's looking at you, Yale). CNN.com reports that about 75 percent of college students admit to engaging in a hook-up, and even if they're not, they know somebody who is. (Not exactly shocking when you force a bunch of hormonally charged young adults under one roof together.)

Taking a stand on one-night stands

So what do you do when you're over hooking up and ready to look for something a little deeper? The Love Fidelity Network (LFN) has experienced steady growth all over the country as it continues to spread the message and provide students with an alternative to casual sex. The nonprofit organization has gained a presence on multiple campuses through the promotion of marriage, abstinence, and the ever-elusive true love amongst college students. Though this may appear like a tough crowd to conquer, the tides seem to be changing. LFN and other organizations like True Love Revolution are attracting followers in droves as more and more students start to examine the value of conventional dating and long-term relationships.

Celebrities are also speaking out about the dangers of hooking up and what it can do to your self-esteem. Kelly Clarkson's feminine anthem "I Do Not Hook Up" says it all, while Lady Gaga has taken a more direct approach. In a recent interview, the singer stated that she was embracing abstinence after experiencing some serious hook-up action during her college years. "It's not really cool any more to have sex all the time. It's cooler to be strong and independent," she insists.

While the rate of sexually transmitted diseases on college campuses is rising, and the number of men and women who actively perpetuate hooking up seems overwhelming, conservative forces are gaining ground as they continue to encourage the search for true love and meaningful relationships. Some say it is empowering to own and wager one's sexuality; others argue that reserving your sexuality for one person is the end all be all. Bottom line when it comes to dating? Stay true to you, first and foremost. And the rest, as they say, will follow…

BUILDING YOUR NETWORK

Last but not least of the important relationships you will have in college are the ones that you establish as a part of your network for school and life. From professors to mentors to internship advisors to alums you meet at networking events, you may not even know it, but you are building a network. By taking an extra step in being strategic about how you go about building your network, you can develop some key relationships that can come in handy when looking for an internship or even a coveted job.

Let's take a moment to create a plan for the network relationships you will seek during school. To get you started, I've filled out a sample plan.

ACTION PLAN: Build My Network

Career goal: Become a lawyer at a nongovernmental organization.

Potential people to meet: Find an alum who works in the legal field and request a phone call.

How? Contact alumni relations department to see if they have an alumni network; attend three pre-law networking events on campus.

Now it's your turn to complete the action plan.

Career goal: _____

Potential people to meet: _____

_____

How? _____

_____

Note: If you run out of space above, no problem! We have extra "Build My Network" Action Plans for you in the back of the guide.

Don't be afraid to reach out to alums who belong to an alumni or career services network. These individuals have signed up because they want to help people like you succeed!

Networking events are extremely useful for building your network even during your freshman year. But if you attend, don't forget to bring a business card! We're serious. All you need to include is your name, academic area, graduation year, and as much contact information as you'd like to provide. This will leave a positive and lasting impression with the people you meet, and give them a way to get in touch long after the event.

FINAL THOUGHTS

From your roommates to mentors to alumni, several new relationships are an important part of your college life. If you develop, nurture, and manage them successfully, you're well on your way to not only getting a grip on your freshman year but also enjoying a fabulous first-year experience and beyond.

CHECKLIST: Relationships

U Chic's essentials for building relationships that will last a lifetime:

- Create a weekly schedule that includes class, study time, and blocks of hours set aside for friends, family, and significant others.

- Adhere to a "separate but equal" policy. When you're studying or in class, turn off your phone. When you're out with your friends, don't obsess about all the tests, exams, or papers you have coming up.

- Make an investment in your social network. It's not enough to text someone or write on their wall (via Facebook). Call, Skype, or set up a weekly "date" with those closest to you.

- Prioritize the people in your life. Don't blow off a phone call with your mom just so you can hang out with the cute guy down the hall. Abusing or ignoring your support network will only hurt you in the end.

- Take the necessary measures to ensure that your romantic relationships don't take priority over everyone else. Love comes and goes, but family and lifelong friendships are forever.

NEXT STEPS

For more information, head to "Sharing Space," "Love Life," and "The College Perks" in *U Chic: The College Girl's Guide to Everything* or www.UniversityChic.com.

CHAPTER 6

Healthy Me

The best thing you can do for yourself in college is take care of your health. Why? Health reasons are often the main culprits for missed classes, missed semesters, bad grades, and, the worst, school dropouts. Follow the advice in this chapter, and you'll be well on your way to college success without a hitch!

Kelly, Indiana University–Purdue University

I wish I would have known that college is difficult sometimes. You are juggling five or six classes and barely sleeping, yet you are supposed to show up to everything on your agenda on time and looking like you aren't stressed. It is tough.

Don't go to college with any expectation at all of it being like a TV show. Sure, there are loads of fun parties; however, it is impossible to party every night and keep advancing to the next grade level. It is just not going to happen, regardless of what you may have heard. Learning this the hard way is an experience, but it is one you probably do not want. Start strong from the beginning; that way you will have less catching up to do later.

COLLEGE HEALTH 101

It's easy to get sick in college since everyone lives in relatively close quarters. Between sharing a bedroom with a stranger and a bathroom with your *entire* floor, infection or (gulp!) infestation can spread pretty quickly. Although a head cold or a sore throat might not propel you into the campus health clinic, you can't be too careful since many symptoms are hard to write off without a doctor's exam.

Mononucleosis: Otherwise known as "mono," this viral infection is spread through saliva or close contact. It starts with feelings of fatigue and flulike symptoms and can quickly snowball into a swollen spleen, high fever, and severe jaundice. Mono can be completely debilitating for students since there's no cure for it besides rest and plenty of fluids, plus it can linger in your system for months and months. If you suspect you or someone you know has mono, your best bet is to avoid contact, clean your eating utensils thoroughly, and keep a large supply of hand sanitizer around at all times.

Meningitis: Each year, the local news is quick to report an outbreak of meningitis at schools around the country for one simple reason: It spreads quickly and the results can be deadly. Symptoms of meningitis include headache, fatigue, a stiff and painful neck, nausea and vomiting, and trouble staying awake. An individual with these symptoms may not suffer from meningitis, so it is important to see a doctor who can provide a proper diagnosis. He or she will likely use a test called a lumbar puncture, also known as a spinal tap. The doctor will extract fluid from your spinal cord and administer tests to see if it contains organisms indicative of the illness.

Once diagnosed, treatment may vary. The more serious strain, bacterial meningitis, requires a hospital stay, but viral meningitis often can be taken care of at home (increased fluid intake, rest, and painkillers to treat headache, fever, or body pain are recommended). Unlike mono, it can be treated with common antibiotics like penicillin or cefotaxime. Most colleges require a meningitis vaccine before moving into the dorms, so make sure to check out your school's website for more details.

Staph Infections: Also known as MRSA, this deadly infection is often picked up via an open cut, nick, or scrape on your body. Common infection sites include sports facilities, gyms, and communal bathrooms. If you notice a pimple, boil, or rash that refuses to heal, seek a doctor ASAP. Many staph infections are drug resistant and can result in death if not treated immediately.

Head Lice: Sharing is caring—just not when it involves parasitic insects that live in your hair. You can decrease your chances of getting lice by not sharing bedding, brushes, clothing, or hats with friends and roommates. While embarrassing and annoying, head lice is easily treatable. Most drugstores and pharmacies offer over-the-counter shampoos and medications that immediately kill lice and nits.

Bed Bugs: The summer of 2010 ushered in a new hysteria in cities and on college campuses all across America: Bed bugs are on the rise and they seem to be popping up everywhere from Ivy League schools to small private colleges as far away as Alaska. While bed bugs can hide for days on end (hiding in headboards is common), the evidence they leave behind is often unmistakable. Bites usually occur in groupings of three along the head, neck, shoulders, and arms. Dark black and red spots on your sheets (the excrement and blood they leave behind after making a meal out of you) are also a telltale sign. If you suspect your dorm room or apartment might be infected, alert your landlord or dorm supervisor *immediately*. Bed bugs spread quickly and are hard to eradicate, so the sooner you tell someone the faster they can respond.

AND DON'T FORGET YOUR BEAUTY REST!

Your mother always said to go to bed early and get plenty of sleep, and now there is plenty of research to back her up. Getting a proper amount of sleep—at least seven to eight hours per night—has been shown to improve academic performance in college students.

However, as you are most likely aware, college provides a unique opportunity for altered sleep habits. You may find yourself up into the wee hours discussing the meaning of life with roommates, not thinking about that 8:00 a.m. class the next day. These times are an important part of the college experience, and you can't always stick to a rigid schedule. So in case you find yourself in need of rest in the middle of the day, there is nothing wrong with a power nap. In fact, it can become one of your best-kept secrets. Taking a mid-afternoon nap during your free time can rejuvenate you for the rest of the day, and get you back on track for the rest of the week. Just remember that you can always be creative and flexible with your schedule.

U Chic Tip!

The "No All-Nighter Rule": Researchers have found that students who pull all-nighters to study get lower exam grades. Make sure to plan your study schedule so you won't feel pressured into pulling an all-nighter.

It also has been shown to have a positive effect on everything from emotional well-being to physical health to productivity and good performance in class. Who would have thought that simply going to bed was so good for you?

Things That Help You Get a Good Night's Sleep Include:

- Having a nighttime routine and a standard bedtime.
- Limiting late nights during the week.
- Staying away from caffeine later in the day.
- Getting exercise daily.
- Staying away from alcohol before bed, as it's been shown to decrease sleep quality.
- Using earplugs or a white-noise machine (especially if you have night-owl roommates or noisy neighbors) to help block out the sound, helping you get a better night's rest.

EXERCISE YOUR WAY TO A BETTER YOU

Exercise is possibly the most beneficial thing you can do for both your body and your mind. Recent groundbreaking research showed that college students who exercised twenty minutes or more per day had a GPA that was 0.4 point higher than those who didn't! There are many other benefits to exercise, which:

- Strengthens your immune system, protecting you from getting sick.
- Improves mental well-being.
- Improves academic performance.
- Reduces stress and anxiety.
- And, as we noted above, improves sleep.

Finding time

As a busy college student, how do you find the time to get exercise? Sure, it's easy to say "I just don't have time to exercise," and occasionally there are days when that is true. However, if you make exercising regularly a priority and *plan* it into your schedule, you'll find that fitting it in has never been easier.

U Chic Tip!

Exercise for stress relief: Whenever you are feeling stressed out, resist the temptation to indulge in comfort food, and go straight to the gym. Don't even give yourself time to think about it—just get your workout clothes on and go. Maybe even call a friend on the way there. This is the best and healthiest way to deal with stress.

Better yet, since exercise reduces stress and improves your energy level, you will be a lot more productive on days that you exercise.

An Exercise Plan

Here are several surefire ways to fit exercise into your busy schedule:

- Include time for exercise in your class schedule at least two or three times a week, and treat it just like one of your classes.

- Set out your workout clothes the night before, so you won't be searching your closet for that left shoe in the morning.

- If your gym is on campus, pack your workout clothes and take them to campus to save time.

- Find a workout partner! You are less likely to skip a workout if someone is depending on you to be there.

- Join a running club or play an intramural sport—these add variety, are guaranteed fun, and provide a way to meet people.

What's right for me?

Wondering what type of exercise is the best? Truth be told, the best type of exercise is the one that you enjoy the most and, therefore, will continue to do long-term. So if you prefer a quick cardio boost, plan running, jogging, or biking excursions on campus or in the community. If working out with friends makes it easier for you to stay engaged, find a workout buddy at the gym or join a team sport like basketball or Ultimate Frisbee.

How often should you exercise and for how long?

It is important that the exercise is vigorous (gets you breathing hard) and that you do it for at least twenty

Your school will have a variety of intramural team sport options to choose from, and some schools even allow you to get course credit for taking a sports-focused class.

to thirty minutes several times per week. Adding in weight-training a couple times per week can help tone your muscles and add variety to your routine. But don't forget this essential tip: Be sure to pick activities that you will stick with through the long term!

Now that you've thought through some of your fitness goals, let's work through an action plan that will keep you happy and healthy in college!

ACTION PLAN: Healthy Me

List three fitness goals for your first year of college, and try be as specific as possible (i.e., run in a race—5K, 10K, or even further; complete a season on an intramural team; improve strength/endurance; etc.):

1. _____

2. _____

3. _____

List at least three forms of exercise you enjoy or would like to try that will help you reach the goals you've listed above (i.e., running, biking, swimming, strength training, kickboxing, intramural team sports, etc.):

1. _____

2. _____

3. _____

List as many things you can think of that will help you meet these goals (i.e., find a workout partner, get good running shoes, schedule workouts into your day, etc.):

_____

_____

_____

_____

Finally, plan out a weekly schedule for the semester that incorporates the fitness goals you listed:

Day	Activity	Length of time	Things that will help me meet this goal
Monday			
Tuesday			
Wednesday			
Thursday			
Friday			
Saturday			
Sunday			

Note: If you run out of space above, no problem! We have extra "Healthy Me" Action Plans for you in the back of the guide.

WEIGHING THE ISSUES

Of course we couldn't talk about health and exercise without addressing the "dreaded" Freshman 15. What's to blame for this college phenomenon and how can you avoid it? The answer is actually pretty straightforward.

First, it's important that you do not become too concerned about what the scale is telling you. It's a scientific fact that your weight will fluctuate by several pounds throughout the week for various reasons. Becoming obsessed with the numbers on the scale can lead to other problems.

Instead, it's better to focus on being healthy, feeling good, and choosing healthy habits each day. It is true that lack of exercise, poor diet, stress, and poor sleep patterns all contribute to weight gain. They all go hand in hand. For instance, if you are well-rested, you will be more likely to eat a healthy breakfast and exercise sometime during the day. This helps relieves stress and prevents you from making bad food choices throughout the day. See what I mean about them all going hand-in-hand? The trick is not to focus on just one thing, but to focus on what we like to call the Big Three: diet, exercise, and sleep. We've already covered the last two, so let's take a look at diet and nutrition

Nutritional balance

Most likely you've heard the expression "You are what you eat." If you eat poorly, then you will likely feel poorly during the day. On the flip side, if you eat healthy food, you're going to feel healthy, too.

One of the best things you can do for yourself is to eat breakfast, especially protein. Options with plenty of protein and low saturated fat include low-fat yogurt and milk, egg whites, peanut butter, and certain types of health bars. Taking a daily vitamin is also a good idea.

Empty calories, empty you

For the rest of your day, it is important to stay away from empty calories, such as soda, candy, and alcohol. One good way to do this is to first drink a glass of water whenever you have the urge to buy a soda or grab a beer. Often you are just thirsty, and water is what you really need anyway. Sure, you still might eventually have that soft drink or beer, but you aren't as likely to have as much if you've been drinking water. By following the "Glass of Water Rule," you will avoid countless empty calories and stay well hydrated.

Get Your Snack on!

Sadly, few dining halls are open twenty-four hours a day, and ordering a pizza just isn't a possibility at 4:00 a.m. when you're right in the middle of cramming for that big organic chemistry midterm. What can you eat in a pinch? Pick up one of these healthy snack alternatives!

1. **Protein bars:** Keep your energy up and the calories down with a quick protein bar. They're individually wrapped so you won't overeat, plus they're portable (in case you sleep through your alarm and need to eat breakfast en-route to class).

2. **Yogurt and low-fat granola:** Although granola can be a secret calorie bomb, a low-fat version eaten in small portions delivers just the right amount of carbs and healthy grains. Mix about a quarter cup of granola with half a cup of your favorite yogurt, and you've got a great snack anytime of the day!

3. **Dried fruit:** Dried apples and banana chips (read your labels carefully—some can be high in fat!) or Craisins cranberries don't need to be refrigerated and are easy to store in your room. The natural sugars in each can give you an extra burst of energy when you're dragging butt or craving a candy fix.

4. **Hot tea:** Step away from that soda machine! A cup of organic tea offers a safe amount of caffeine for late-night studying, is calorie-free, and boosts immunity—key on many college campuses where bathrooms are often shared, and flu season can stop the average student in his or her tracks.

5. **Whole-grain cereal:** Starving and looking for a fast fix? Cereal is a great food to stash in your dorm room and eat late at night with or without milk. Kashi cereals are often healthy *and* a delicious option, as are Barbara's Organic Cereal varieties. Tempted to add some sugar? Just sweeten it up with a bit of vanilla-flavored soy milk.

6. **Carrots and hummus:** Carrots are a super-food, which means they have more vitamins than paler veggies and are seriously low cal! Hummus is full of protein, which helps with memory retention and concentration. Pair the two together and you have the perfect study snack!

When it comes to eating lunch and dinner, sometimes the best advice is the simplest advice—"Plan your meals ahead." Skipping lunch is a bad idea because you will hit an energy low in the afternoon and lose focus. It's bad for your grades and bad for your mood. This often leads to buying a soft drink, coffee drink, or candy bar to give you a quick boost, which is a bad habit to get into.

We all know that it is easy to order way too much food when we are starving, and then feel obligated to finish it all, leaving us feeling stuffed and in a food coma for the next couple of hours. By planning meals, you will not be in this situation as often, and can have proper portions and a healthier diet.

Eating disorders

"Disordered eating" is becoming a big issue on college campuses. In fact, researchers have found that one in ten college women may fit the clinical criteria for an eating disorder such as anorexia or bulimia, and up to one in three women may have some form of "disordered eating," such as using diet pills and laxatives, or occasionally bingeing and purging.

There are many signs you can look for that may indicate an eating disorder, and if you see these in friends or yourself, seek help.

Here are some possible signs and symptoms of an eating disorder:

- Sudden dramatic weight loss.

- Frequent bathroom trips during or following meals.

- Loss of a normal menstrual cycle.

- Obsession with weight and calorie contents of foods.

- Use of laxatives or diet pills.

- Hair loss, hair thinning, or pale appearance.

- Isolation, depression, fatigue, and other similar symptoms can be related to an eating disorder.

Suspect that a friend might be experiencing disordered eating? Try bringing up the issue in a nonjudgmental way, such as, "I noticed you haven't been eating much. If you ever want to talk about things, I'm always here for you." This can then lead to the suggestion of seeking professional help. Anyone with an eating disorder should be encouraged to seek professional help, which can be lifesaving in the most serious cases.

ALCOHOL AND DRUGS

One of the biggest health issues on college campuses is binge drinking, which very often results in decisions that people regret the next day, and occasionally results in serious illness or even death.

After a night of heavy drinking, you will rarely hear anyone say, "I'm really glad I drank so much last night, because this hangover feels great and I can't even remember what I did." But since drinking impairs judgment, it is harder to stop after you have had a drink or two, especially if you are continually being offered drinks at a party. So it's important to plan ahead to avoid binge drinking. For example, follow the Glass of Water Rule—have a glass of water or nonalcoholic beverage for every other drink. This will keep you better hydrated and reduce the ill effects and extra calories of alcohol.

Drinking and Drugs: A Few Tips to Consider

- If you are under twenty-one and choose to drink, remember that in addition to putting your health at risk, you are taking the risk of being arrested. Today it is simple for employers to do background checks, and an alcohol offense on your record looks irresponsible and could potentially hurt your employment or internship prospects.

- Some signs of alcohol abuse include *increased tolerance, blackouts, drinking alone, and drinking to deal with stress*. If you see these occurring in yourself or others, it is better to seek help now than wait for the problem to worsen.

- If you plan to go out drinking, set your limits beforehand with a friend, and pledge to watch out for each other.

- When it comes to drugs, be wary of a new problem facing college campuses today: prescription drug abuse. There has been a rise in stimulant abuse (e.g., Adderall, Ritalin) as well as painkillers (e.g., Percocet, Vicodin) and antianxiety drugs (e.g., Xanax, Valium) in people who are not prescribed these drugs for legitimate medical reasons.

- Some students are under the false assumption that stimulants such as Ritalin and Adderall will help their grades by getting them through all-nighters and marathon study sessions, when the reality is that having good study, exercise, and sleep habits in the first place is the real secret to getting good grades. We already covered the fact that all-nighters and cramming result in lower grades, so don't let yourself be fooled that stimulants are going to help you.

- Abuse of painkillers and antianxiety medications is just as serious as alcohol and illegal drug abuse, and you should take similar precautions.

- Drugs can contain toxic chemicals, and you can never be sure what is in them.

- If you get caught with drugs, you can face jail time, and can usually kiss a variety of potential careers goodbye (law school, medical school, government work, etc.).

- Car wrecks, suicide, and falls are often associated with drugs.

- Drugs can ruin friendships, your looks, your health, and your financial stability.

- When it comes to drugs, whether illegal drugs or prescription drugs being used illegally, it is best to stay far, far away.

SEX ED

Another important health area for college students is sexual activity. The average college student today knows more about safe sex than students did forty years ago. But it never hurts to brush up on this knowledge. To test your basic knowledge of sexual health, try this pop quiz:

POP QUIZ: Sex Ed 101

1. What is the most effective form of birth control?

2. What is the proper technique for putting on a condom?

3. How effective is the birth control pill at preventing pregnancy?

4. Is it possible to get sexually transmitted infections (STDs) from oral sex?

5. How can you tell if someone else has an STD?

If you know the answers to these questions, then you get an A+. Missed a few? Here's the crib sheet:

Answer to 1: Abstinence is the best form of birth control and the best form of protection from STDs. This is obvious, but needs to be said.

Answer to 2: Improper condom use is more common than you would think and has caused plenty of unwanted pregnancies and STDs. Knowing how a condom should be put on is a simple way to protect your health. Though the details on condom application are out of the scope of this book, you can find more info online, at sites such as www.plannedparenthood.com.

Answer to 3: For sexually active women, taking the birth control pill properly is generally over 99 percent effective for preventing pregnancy.

Answer to 4: Yes, it is possible. Herpes transmission is probably the most common risk of oral sex, especially during an outbreak when skin lesions are present. For more information, just check out any school's student health resource center online (Brown and Stanford cover this particular topic well).

Answer to 5: There is no way to tell for sure. Educate yourself about signs and symptoms of STDs. These include abnormal vaginal discharge, pain or burning with urination or intercourse, genital sores or warts, vaginal itching, and others. Condom use is a must at all times, just like wearing your seatbelt is.

As there is no way to tell for sure if a potential partner has an STD, you have every right to (and should!) ask about his sexual history and whether or not he has been tested.

STDs: The risks

There are two types of STDs: bacterial and viral strains. Bacterial are the easiest to treat, while viral ones like HIV are untreatable and can only be managed through long-term lifestyle changes and medication. The problem is, not every STD comes with obvious symptoms, so it can be hard to diagnose yourself. This is why regular testing and using condoms are key.

The three most common types of STDs are as follows:

Human Papilloma Virus: Also known as HPV or genital warts, this STD is by far the most common on college campuses across American. While the recent HPV immunization shot is readily available to most young women, diagnosing it after the fact can be tricky since it can lie dormant in your body for years and years. Common symptoms include wartlike bumps or sores on or near the genital region. If you suspect you may be infected, you need to go to a doctor right away—HPV can cause infertility, cervical cancer, and increase your chances of HIV if left untreated.

Chlamydia: Considered the second most common STD among college students, this yucky virus is transmitted via vaginal, anal, and, yes, even oral sex. According to The Centers for Disease Control, about one in ten teenage girls and young women have or will test positive for chlamydia. While this STD can also result in a symptom-free infection, the fact that it can cause you to become permanently sterile should be enough incentive to go in for regular screenings at your campus health clinic or doctor's office.

Genital Herpes: Often spread by genital contact, genital herpes is one of those STDs a lot of people have but fail to realize until they accidentally spread it to another partner. Symptoms usually include bumps and sores around the genital region and can extend to fatigue or flulike symptoms. If you're feeling run-down and notice something unusual going on "down there," don't wait to see a doctor. While untreatable, outbreaks can be managed with medication and lifestyle adjustments, like getting more sleep, avoiding stress, staying healthy, and eating a balanced diet.

What to do when safe sex proves not-so-safe?

The most important fact you need to know about emergency contraception, or "the morning after pill" is that it is *not* a regular method of birth control and doesn't prevent sexually transmitted diseases. The pill (a.k.a. Plan B) is currently available for women seventeen years or older without a prescription at most pharmacies in the United States. Plan B will stop pregnancy in about 98 percent of cases if administered correctly and taken within seventy-two hours. This pill should only be taken if a condom breaks during sex, your regular birth control routine has been disrupted, or if you are sexually assaulted.

When it comes to your sexual health, here's the bottom line: Remember that your campus has several great resources at your disposal, including the campus health clinic. Don't think twice about using them if you have any questions or concerns.

SAFETY MATTERS

We can't move on to the next chapter without addressing safety issues on- and off-campus. But first, it's important to know the facts. According to the U.S. Department of Justice, young women between the ages of sixteen and twenty-four are most at risk for being raped. Add in the fact that over 81 percent of college women don't report assaults, and the numbers sound even more alarming. And these statistics don't include the thousands of students who are robbed or assaulted each year. First, we want to say that, no matter what, assault or rape is never the victim's fault. With that being said, there are still things you can do to help keep yourself safer and minimize your risk. The best way to keep this from ever happening to you? Protect yourself by having a plan for staying safe.

POP QUIZ: What's My Safety Quotient?

Are you putting yourself at risk? Test your safety quotient and find out.

1. **You're studying late at the library with a bunch of classmates when they all decide to hit the bar afterward. You have too much to do, so you:**

   A.   Walk out with them and then head back to the dorms by yourself.

   B.   Have them drop you off at the nearest bus stop.

   C.   Call campus security and request a ride back to your dorm.

2. **It's Friday night, you're at a frat party, and a really cute guy offers you a drink. Your response?**

   A.   "Thanks! I totally needed that."

   B.   "You take it. I'm going to grab a fresh beer from the keg."

   C.   "Bummer. I'd love to drink that, but I'm the official DD for the night."

3. **You break up with your boyfriend and he starts to go overboard calling, texting, and following you around everywhere. How do you handle it?**

   A.   Ask his best friend to talk to him.

   B.   Let all your friends know what's going on and set up phone check-in times so you're in constant contact with them.

   C.   Go to campus security and report that he's harassing you.

4. **Your roommate's b-day party at the local bar has kinda gotten out of hand, and everyone has either had too much to drink or they're in the process of lining up a hot hook-up. The cute guy**

from your calc class (the one you talk to all the time) offers you a ride home. You say:

A.   OK.

B.   Maybe some other day.

C.   No way.

5. **No clean clothes plus a weekend away with your friends equals a late-night laundry session all by yourself. There's no cell phone signal in the room, and everyone in the dorms is asleep. What do you take to occupy your time?**

A.   Your iPod.

B.   Your laptop so you can catch up on your TV shows.

C.   Your roommate. There's no way you're sitting down there all alone.

Mostly As: You may have book smarts, but your street smarts definitely need work. Walking home alone, accepting rides from strangers, putting yourself in vulnerable situations—these all add up to you possibly being hurt or victimized. Assess each situation carefully *before* a split-second decision changes the course of your life forever.

Mostly Bs: It's obvious that you have most of the big safety stuff down, but you may need a refresher course. Don't be afraid to speak up and ask for a ride or call campus security if you feel uncomfortable or feel you may be in danger. Trust your instincts—they won't steer you wrong.

Mostly Cs: Safety might as well be your middle name, but be careful not to tread into the land of paranoia. Not everyone is out to get you. Just be careful and go with your gut. After all, college *is* supposed to be a fun learning experience.

How did you do? No matter where you currently fall on the safety spectrum, you can always change that by taking action.

Here are some additional tips for staying safe on campus:

- Know how to contact public safety and the police department: Keep these emergency numbers close to you and program them into your cell phone. Better yet, memorize them!

- Subscribe to the campus mass notification system.

- Know the campus. Familiarize yourself with the layout of the campus during the day and after dark (with a friend, of course!).

- Know which sidewalks are adequately lit or not.

- Take a self-defense course, such as a Rape Aggression Defense (R.A.D.) course if it is offered.

- Lock all doors and windows every time you leave your room/apartment/home, even if you plan to be gone for just a minute.

- Keep house and car keys on separate rings.

- Do not lend your keys to service/maintenance people you do not know well.

- Always ask service/maintenance people to identify themselves before allowing them to enter your room/apartment/home.

- Get to know your neighbors so you can help each other.

- Do not keep large sums of money, jewelry, or valuable items in plain view in your room/apartment/home.

- When out of town, set radios, lights, and televisions on timers.

- If you are living off campus, leave spare keys with trusted neighbors, not under a doormat or in a flower planter.

- Try to avoid entering elevators occupied by strangers. If you are waiting for an elevator with a stranger, stand away from the door to avoid being pushed inside.

- Get off on the next floor if you feel uneasy. Hit the alarm button if you are accosted on an elevator.
- Report any broken or malfunctioning locks to the facilities department.

FINAL THOUGHTS

Remember, your most *important* relationship is the one you have with yourself. Exercising, eating well, getting enough sleep, and being responsible about alcohol, drugs, and sex are important if you want to create a healthy balance between school and your social life.

CHECKLIST: Healthy Me

U Chic's essentials for staying healthy and happy in college:

- Pick a bedtime and stick to it.
- Schedule at least three to five workouts per week. Remember that exercise is the best thing you can do for your grades and your body.
- Find a workout partner or join an intramural sports club. This will add variety to your exercise and keep you motivated.
- Plan your workouts ahead of time by making them a part of your weekly schedule. Whether packing your own lunch, deciding when and where to eat on campus, or setting out your gym clothes in advance, you are taking a big step toward great health in college and life!
- If you suspect that your friends or even you may be suffering from a major health concern like the ones discussed in this chapter, refer them to or head to your campus health clinic right away.

NEXT STEPS

For more information, head to "Healthy and Happy" and "Surviving Temptation Island" in *U Chic: The College Girl's Guide to Everything* or www.UniversityChic.com.

CHAPTER 7

Frosh Finances

W hen it comes to getting started in college, does it seem like the only thing your friends and the media ever talk about is the "dreaded" Freshman 15? We say forget that fifteen pounds. What you should be most concerned about is the other fifteen—the potential $15,000+ debt burden that more and more college students are graduating with these days. This chapter is all about helping you avoid this unnecessary baggage. The secret? You need to have a plan—and budget—in place.

THE REALITY

You're on your own for the first time in your life, and suddenly you are juggling all of your own finances. Although it may seem like you have a large amount of money from financial aid, loans, and financial support from your family, this money goes fast.

Here's the harsh reality about college—it's expensive. According to an advisor at a major university, more students drop out of college due to credit card debt than to academic failure. Don't let this be you. The best way to prevent this is to adopt a spending plan early in your first semester, and stick to it. If you think you're too young for a sound financial plan, you're wrong. There is no better time than now for you to learn these important skills that will last you a lifetime. Before we launch into the discussion, here's an exercise to determine your "budget style."

POP QUIZ: What's Your Budget Style?

Often times, students leave for college without a strong sense of how to manage their finances. Sure, Mom and Dad have always been there to feed you, clothe you, and keep a roof over your head, but what happens when *you're* the one in the driver's seat? Take this quiz to determine your saving and spending style.

1. **How many times have you been guilty of using that "emergency" credit card your parents gave you before you went away to school?**

   A. Um, a lot.

   B. Not often, but enough that my parents have threatened to take it away from me.

   C. Rarely.

2. **Be honest: Which of these best describes your monthly priority list?**

   A. Food, clothing, going out, concerts, and other "must-haves" like movie rentals and iTunes downloads.

   B. Food, bills, going out, eating out, and weekly trips to the mall.

   C. Food, bills, laundry, going out, and saving the rest.

3. **If your checking/savings account could talk, what would it say?**

   A. "Feed me! I'm starving!"

   B. "Come on, didn't you just buy twenty rolls of toilet paper last month?"

   C. "Keep it up, and I might just have to introduce you to my friend, Money Marketing Account!"

4. **By the time the end of the month rolls around, you're usually:**

   A. Begging your parents for an advance and living on ramen noodles.

B. Feeling guilty about that pair of leather boots you just *had* to have and hoping you can squeak by so your parents don't find out.

C. Annoyed that all of your friends are hitting you up for loans.

5. **Do the terms "overdraft fee," "late fee," and "credit score" keep you up at night?**

A. All the time! You're constantly stressing about paying your bills on time.

B. Sometimes, but not often.

C. No way! You've got your spending on lockdown.

Mostly As: Step away from that ATM machine! You're not in a good place right now, and spending even *more* money is only going to make it worse. Managing your finances is what separates the grown-ups from the kids, and if you want to be treated like an adult, it's time to act like one. Make a concerted effort to track your spending so you're aware of where your money is going and make an honest assessment of what's necessary and what's not. Did you *really* need a new outfit? Was going to that concert more important than paying your phone bill on time? Crunch the numbers and create an action plan that will put you in the black—*not* the red.

Mostly Bs: You know how to manage your money…you just feel guilty sometimes when you make an expensive purchase that forces you to either ask your parents for money or scrimp to get through the end of the month. If something is telling you *not* to blow your cash, *listen*! Impulse spending can easily derail you and can lead to poor spending habits and bad credit in the future. Resist the urge to splurge and concentrate on saving instead.

Mostly Cs: Congrats! You're wise beyond your years when it comes to being a smart financial planner. Understanding the need for delayed gratification is an important aspect of responsible spending. This kind of thinking will only aid you in the future when it comes time for buying a car, securing a mortgage, or (drum roll, please) paying off your student loans on time. Sure, it kinda sucks when your friends are all out shopping or partying, but trust us, the long-term benefits far outweigh a cute outfit and a night on the town with your girls.

CREDIT CARDS 101

Does it seem like everywhere you turn, a credit card company is encouraging you to sign up? Swipe, swipe, swipe. Paying for things never seemed easier. You buy clothes, gas, beer, pizza, and concert tickets, and you party.

But before you know it, you find yourself unable to pay your credit card bills, or you have no money left to buy books for your classes. Or you may get along just fine for a while, only to have a rude awakening at some point. Even worse? You end up at graduation with a diploma and thousands of dollars of unnecessary—and crippling—debt in hand.

Here's how you can minimize and, possibly, avoid this altogether in school.

First, credit and debit cards are an unavoidable part of modern life. From books to copying fees, there are expenses you cannot avoid in college, and a credit card can help out in these cases. Also, credit cards are an essential piece of building good credit, which can help out later in life when you want to buy a home or new car. The trick is to take steps to minimize the potential for debt trouble down the road. Here are several suggestions on what you can do, courtesy of Jason Alderman at Visa Inc.:[1]

- Look for a bank or credit union that charges no monthly usage fee, requires no minimum balance, and has conveniently located ATMs so you don't rack up foreign ATM charges.

- Enter all transactions in the check register or use a digital tool like Mint .com and review the account online weekly to know when deposits, checks, purchases, and automatic payments have cleared.

- Avoid writing checks to pay off credit cards or making debit card transactions unless the current balance will cover them—such transactions often clear instantaneously.

---

1 "Credit 101 for Your College Freshman," *Huffington Post*, http://www.huffingtonpost.com/jason-alderman/credit-101-for-your-colle_b_678798.html, August 11, 2010.

- Banks and credit unions now must ask customers whether they want to opt into overdraft protection plans for ATM and most debit card transactions (but not for personal checks and automatic transactions like monthly bill payments). We highly recommend that you consider adding a protection plan, as overdrafts can be expensive—up to $30 or more per transaction.

- Alternatively, ask if the bank will link your checking account to a savings or other account to avoid overdraft charges.

- Ask for free text or email alerts when your balance drops below a certain level, checks or deposits clear, or payments are due.

Credit card companies and marketers know how to tempt your desire for instant gratification. By having a budget in place and sticking to it, you are putting yourself one step closer to achieving your lifelong dreams.

AUTOMATE IT!

Other tricks for avoiding debt? Thanks to modern technology, you have the ability to set up automated systems that can work to your advantage. Here are several things you can do.

Working part-time? Set up your paycheck to deposit directly to your account.

Have monthly phone, credit card, rent, or utility bills that you're in charge of? Plan to have these payments directly deducted from your account each month, and you'll never have to pay a late fee again! Contact these companies to find out how to do this.

If you make enough money that can be saved, set up an automatic deduction from your checking account to a savings account in your name.

And if you're really money savvy, you can even set up a retirement fund to receive these extra earnings. Visit a stock brokerage firm website—like fidelity.com, vanguard.com, or schwab.com—for more information.

BUT OH THOSE TEMPTATIONS

Girls night out. Spring break in Cancun. A fabulous Betsy Johnson dress for spring formal. When you're on a budget, temptations will present themselves, guaranteed. The trick is to be able to categorize these items into those you must have and those you can do without.

EXERCISE: My Money Habits

Am I managing my money wisely? Answer these questions to determine your current money habits. Check yes or no.

1. Have you ever bought an item of clothing and decided when you got home that it wasn't for you, but failed to return it to the store in time to get your money back?
   YES____ **NO**____

2. Do you continually return DVDs, books, or other items late, incurring late fees?
   YES____ **NO**____

3. Do you rarely shop at discount, usually paying full price for the latest fashion?
   YES____ **NO**____

4. Do you send your clothes out for dry cleaning when all they need is a quick once-over with an iron?
   YES____ **NO**____

5. Are parking tickets a common occurrence for you?
   YES____ **NO**____

6. Do you borrow things from friends and fail to return them?
   YES____ **NO**____

7. Do you own several gadgets—iPod, iPhone, Blackberry, etc.—when all you really need is one?
   YES____ **NO**____

If you've checked more yes's than no's, then you're on the way to spending more money than you have each semester, leading you down the debt path of no return. Let's shape up these money habits now with a new approach.

Take a moment to go through each yes you checked and write down why you think you do that *and* what steps you can take to change this behavior. This is an important first step in getting yourself on more solid financial ground:

_____

_____

_____

_____

_____

_____

_____

_____

_____

By understanding your bad habits now, you are well on your way to financial bliss.

COLLEGE BUDGET

The best thing you can do for yourself at the very beginning of your college career is to take whatever remaining money you have after paying tuition—whether in the form of loans, grants, your own money, work on campus, or a combination of these—and then set a budget. It may seem a little too soon to make a budget right when you arrive on campus, but it is essential that you take these important first steps to get on a sound financial path. Here's a step-by-step process to help you get started:

1. **How much money is coming in?** It may be money from home, part-time work, or from your savings.

2. **Track your spending.** Take your starting amount, and subtract each and every purchase you make, including those morning latte or late-night donut runs. And don't forget to track use of your campus meal plan. Did you spend money at Subway for lunch when you could have gone to the dorm cafeteria?

3. **Create the budget.** Once you have tracked what comes in and what goes out over a couple of weeks, it's now time to make a budget. Better yet? You are now in great position to cut what you can and keep what you must. For instance, maybe you don't need that monthly manicure (you can do this at home). You might find more money in your budget if you cut out unnecessary expenses.

Here's a sample budget form to get you started. Turn to page 162 for complete forms that you can fill in on your own.

ACTION PLAN: The College Budget

SEMESTER BUDGET WORKSHEET FOR COLLEGE STUDENTS

CATEGORY	SEMESTER BUDGET	SEMESTER ACTUAL	SEMESTER DIFFERENCE
INCOME:			
From Jobs			
From Parents			
From Student Loans			
From Scholarships			
From Other Financial Aid			
Miscellaneous Income			
INCOME SUBTOTAL			
EXPENSES:			
Rent or Room & Board			
Utilities			

CATEGORY	SEMESTER BUDGET	SEMESTER ACTUAL	SEMESTER DIFFERENCE
Telephone			
Groceries			
Toiletries/Makeup			
Car Payment/Transportation			
Insurance			
Gasoline/Oil			
Repairs and Maintenance			
Entertainment			
Eating Out/Vending			
Tuition			
Books			
School Fees			
Computer Expenses			
Miscellaneous Expenses			
EXPENSES SUBTOTAL			
NET INCOME (INCOME LESS EXPENSES)			

If an expense is incurred more or less often than once each semester, convert it to a semester amount when filling out the budget. For instance, an auto expense that is billed every year would be converted to a semester by dividing the amount in half.

It's also important to point out that, when totaling your net income, the goal is to not end up in the hole or with a negative number. If you did, go back and adjust your budget amounts, so you come out on top.

Note: If you run out of space above, no problem! We have extra "College Budget" sheets for you in the back of the guide.

When filling out your budget, be honest with yourself about where you can allow yourself to spend and where you should save. That way, you'll have more money for the things you need and, of course, those that you really want to do (like that fabulous spring break trip with friends).

TO WORK OR NOT TO WORK

We've talked about credit cards, bad money habits, potential temptations, and how to set a budget. There is one last crucial issue to tackle—to work or not to work.

Earnings from a job undoubtedly help alleviate some of the financial struggles you face in college. And it never hurts to have a few extra bucks each month for the fun things you want to do. However, holding down a job while going to school full-time can do more harm than good if you're not careful. Let's take a moment to think through the issues.

First: Why work? Of course, the extra money will give some padding to the budget you created above. But studies have also found that part-time employment has beneficial effects. For instance, an on-campus research position may spark an interest in a new line of study or even a potential career down the road. It can even improve your chances of landing a job post-college. And since part-time work usually only fills downtime in your schedule when you would be doing things like watching TV, working shouldn't prevent you from having that rewarding college experience that everyone wants. Even more interesting, students who work fewer than ten hours per week have slightly higher GPAs than students who don't.

On the other hand, full-time employment may impair your academic performance. Studies have found that working more than thirty-five hours per week could have a negative impact on students' grades. Full-time work can also limit your class scheduling options, from the number of classes you can take at one time to individual course choices. Also, students who work full time are more likely to drop out of school.

So how much is too much when it comes to working full time? Actually, it is unclear at what point student employment moves from being beneficial to being counterproductive. Given that uncertainty, we're not trying to talk you out of full-time work. We're here to provide the facts and support you in whatever decision you make. But you have to agree: The difference between graduating from college and not graduating from college is pretty significant, and one you should definitely take into consideration when deciding whether to work, and how much to work.

FINAL THOUGHTS

Now that we've gotten through the basics of frosh finances, think you've got what it takes to make a budget and stick to it? With the tools we went through above and a foolproof budget in hand, we think you are. One thing you are certain not to walk away from college with is a burdensome debt load. Three cheers for that!

CHECKLIST: Frosh Finances

U Chic's essentials for avoiding major college debt:

- Make a semester budget and stick to it. By keeping your money in line with your goals, you are preventing yourself from being burdened with debt post-college.

- Automate your finances as much as possible through direct deposits for earnings from your job or automatic deductions from your account each month to pay bills. This will ensure that your payments are on time and covered, helping you build good credit that will last a lifetime.

- Avoid those college temptations to spend by planning ahead for how you will deal with them. Do you have a friend who always wants to go out and party several days during the week? Make it known to him or her that you're watching your bills and that you can only afford once-a-week outings (if that's the case), and your friend will get the hint, giving you fewer excuses to spend.

- When deciding whether to work, make sure that it's in line with your goals for school. If you think you'll be spending too much time at work, leaving little room for study or fun, then you might want to consider another less burdensome employment opportunity.

- Practice good money habits now, and you'll have them for life!

NEXT STEPS

For more information, head to "Money Matters" in *U Chic: The College Girl's Guide to Everything* or www.UniversityChic.com.

CHAPTER 8

Career Queen

I n chapter 5, we discussed the importance of building your network of contacts from the first day you step foot on campus. That is true for everything about getting a jump start on your career in college. If you want to be a "Career Queen," someone who is doing what she loves full time and getting paid for it, it can only be achieved if you start working toward it from day one. By starting early, you're able to map out a plan, secure those coveted internships, and ultimately place yourself at the head of the pack when it comes to landing that full-time position post-college.

"But wait!" you say. "Graduation is *years* away. Why do I need to stress about this now?"

Ask anyone who's graduated from college, and they'll say the same thing—graduation comes faster than you can imagine. You definitely don't want to be the girl who has to move home to live with her parents because you haven't secured a job after college. To prevent that from ever happening to you, start your career planning early…as soon as *now*.

WHAT'S MY CALLING?

If you're unsure what you want to do post-college, take a skills assessment quiz. As we recommended in chapter 1, Gallup's StrengthsQuest program will help you figure out potential career tracks and professions that are perfect for you. Many schools have adopted it as an official part of the curriculum. If your school hasn't, run an online search on "StrengthsQuest" to get more information.

Once you've got a career track in mind, it's time to start building your academic schedule around these interests and getting involved with related activities on campus. By aligning your studies and campus involvement with your career goals, you are well on your way to being a Career Queen.

SHOULD I PICK A MAJOR BASED ON MY CAREER INTERESTS?

Most professional work opportunities that don't require graduate school training— like engineering or accounting—require a B.S. in that particular area of study. For those of you on more general career tracks like journalism, who don't know what you want to do post-college, or who are at a liberal arts–focused school, it is completely fine for you to pursue an unrelated area of study. In fact, that's what makes college great—the opportunity to explore a wide range of major and career options.

Just remember that at some point, preferably sooner rather than later, you need to be honing in on an area of study so you can, at the very least, graduate on time. Also, if you're not pursuing a degree that's directly related to your dream job, try to pack your schedule with courses that provide some type of exposure to that particular career. How else will you know if that's the right one for you? And when you start going on internship or job interviews, you'll have something to refer back to when the hiring manager would like more information on your background and experience. Your classroom projects and papers can go miles in helping prove or show your passion for a particular job.

WHEN TO START THE INTERNSHIP/JOB HUNT?

The last key pieces of the career-building puzzle are internships or part-time work. In fact, work experience is so important that we'll pretty much spend the rest of this chapter on this topic alone.

Before we get started, read how one student snagged her dream internship.

Victoria, Quinnipiac University

After visiting my academic department and meeting with my advisor, I soon learned that I would not be getting an internship unless I pursued the opportunity myself. So when I decided I wanted to work for a newspaper over summer break, I sent out many emails, marketing myself and my writing.

When I got very few responses from that method, I went to a journalism job fair at a college four hours away. The snow was about two feet deep that day, and as I was walking into the building, I slipped on ice. Still, I made it to my scheduled interview with the managing editor of a newspaper from my home city. I showed her my resume and portfolio, and she asked me if I would be interested in working in the features department. Then she sent me on my way.

I had a feeling I got the internship at that point, but I did not tell anyone because I did not know for sure. But sure enough, two months later, I received an email from the features editor, asking me to come in to meet the staff and get my ID badge. I landed my dream internship!

On my first day, I was assigned to review a new exhibit at the zoo, and I surprisingly had the opportunity to feed a giraffe. My story ended up on page one. I spent the next four months working in the features department and I loved every minute of it. But I did learn that you really have to sell yourself when you are trying to snag a great internship. Internships are competitive to begin with, but if you really want one, you have to go out there and get one. It is definitely worth it.

Moral of the story? When you're on the competitive quest for an internship or job, persistence is often the deciding factor. Of course, don't forget that having a stellar resume and a record of strong academic performance can't hurt either. But your passion and positive attitude will win the day when the right opportunity presents itself. Head to *U Chic: The College Girl's Guide to Everything*'s "College Perks" chapter for more advice on the internship hunt.

SETTING YOUR SEARCH PLAN

We can't emphasize enough that your quest to becoming a Career Queen in college begins day one. That does not mean, however, you need to start sending out your resume for internships that first month. Instead, you need to use the first few months to map out a plan of action. In fact, the single most important thing you can do is to have a plan in hand. That way, you won't have to find yourself scrambling at the last minute for the remaining opportunities that, at the end of the day, are not the perfect fit.

Before we get into that, let's take a moment to go over a timeline for the internship hunt your freshman year.

Internship timeline

It's never too early to start planning for your internship. The entire process, from discovering an opportunity to applying and interviewing for it, can take several months or even a semester.

Here is a general timeline to assist you with the planning process:

PHASE 1: Six months before you want to start your internship:

- Talk with your academic advisor and a career services counselor to find out what internship resources are available on campus.
- Write your resume and cover letter.

- Decide what you would like from your internship. Responsibilities? Compensation? Experience?

- Attend job fairs to find opportunities.

- Start networking with everyone you know.

- Define where you would like to do your internship. City? Corporation? Industry?

- Start researching possibilities. Obtain general information about the company, internship programs, contact people, and deadlines.

PHASE 2: Four to six months out (or sooner, depending on whether the internship in question has an earlier deadline):

- Send out your resume and cover letter.

- Practice your interviewing skills. Schedule a mock interview with your career services office.

PHASE 3: Two to four months out:

- Make sure your application is complete for each company where you would like to intern.

- Interview with employers.

- Send thank-you letters to employers who gave you an opportunity to interview.

PHASE 4:

- Congrats! You've been chosen. Decide on an internship that is best for you, and accept an offer.

Plan to repeat this process as you work your way through college. By completing as many internships or part-time work opportunities as possible, you're increasing the odds of having full-time employment post-college, as many employers prefer to extend job offers to people they know personally and who they are confident can do the job at hand.

Got a feel for how the process works? Now it's time to put your action plan together! Fill in your deadlines below, and check off each item as you knock it out.

ACTION PLAN: Career Queen

PHASE 1:

❏ Talk with your academic advisor and a career services counselor to find out what internship resources are available to you on campus.

Deadline: _____

❏ Write your resume and cover letter.

Deadline: _____

❏ Decide what you would like from your internship. Responsibilities? Compensation? Experience?

Deadline: _____

❏ Attend job fairs to find opportunities.

Deadline: _____

❏ Attend networking events and reach out to anyone who might know of an opportunity.

Deadline: _____

❏ Define where you would like to do your internship. City? Corporation? Industry?

Deadline: _____

❏ Start researching possibilities. Obtain general information about the company, internship programs, contact people, and deadlines.

Deadline: _____

PHASE 2:

❏ Send out your resume and cover letter.

Deadline: _____

❏ Practice your interviewing skills. Schedule a mock interview with your career services office.

Deadline: _____

PHASE 3:

❑ Make sure your application is complete for each company where you would like to intern.

Deadline: _____

❑ Interview with employers.

Deadline: _____

❑ Send thank-you letters to employers who gave you an opportunity to interview.

Deadline: _____

Note: If you run out of space above, no problem! We have extra "Career Queen" Action Plans for you in the back of the guide.

FINAL THOUGHTS

So, you've got your plan and you're ready to roll. Good luck on the hunt! You're going to do great!

CHECKLIST: Career Queen

U Chic's essentials for getting a jump start on your career:

- Start the internship and career hunt as soon as possible your freshman year. Why? The earlier you start, the better. You'll have more choices, and since many internships are awarded on a first come, first served basis, it never hurts to get your application in first.

- Start with a plan. Choose your target jobs wisely, and then tailor your resume and cover letter specifically to their needs. You'll end up with more offers than you can handle.

- College is definitely a time to explore, but don't let the freedom distract you from the ultimate goal at hand—to graduate with a degree that will help you snag that dream job.

- If after your first year in college, you're still unsure what path is right for you, try taking a skills assessment exam like Gallup's StrengthsQuest Program. These exams can help identify your strengths and then help you find career opportunities where you can best put them to work.

- Did you have the worst possible internship experience last summer? Don't ignore it. In fact, let that serve as a potential warning against your chosen career path. What may sound good on a piece of paper or in class may not always be good in reality. If you follow your instincts in school, in your career, and in life, you're more likely to never be let down.

NEXT STEPS

For more information, head to "The College Perks" in *U Chic: The College Girl's Guide to Everything* or www.UniversityChic.com.

CHAPTER 9

The Ultimate Action Plan

New roommates, meal plans, choosing a major. As college freshmen, these are just a few of the pressing and stressing issues you will face. But now that you've made it to the end of the guide with your action plans in hand, you are ready to seize the fabulous college experience that's ahead of you, on your own terms. And if there is any advice I wish I'd had at the beginning of my college career, it is this:

THERE'S NO SUCH THING AS FAILURE, ONLY LIFE LESSONS

You failed an exam. You didn't get into your sorority of choice. Your boyfriend dumped you. So what? Don't get caught up in obsessing about what didn't go your way or what you did wrong. And maybe some of these things weren't right for you anyway. Everything happens for a reason, so focus your energies on how you can change and grow for the better.

To help you plan for the future and to wrap things up, we've created an **Ultimate Action Plan** for you to incorporate all of the planning you've created throughout this guide, so you have a master plan for success in school and in life. Fill it out and keep it close throughout the first year and beyond.

The Ultimate Action Plan

KEY AREAS	WHAT DO I WANT TO ACHIEVE?	HOW AM I GOING TO ACHIEVE IT?	TARGET DATE FOR COMPLETION?
Defining Who You Are			
Class Act			
Campus & Community Maven			
Sorority Life			
Relationships			

KEY AREAS	WHAT DO I WANT TO ACHIEVE?	HOW AM I GOING TO ACHIEVE IT?	TARGET DATE FOR COMPLETION?
Build My Network			
Healthy Me			
The College Budget			
Career Queen			

Note: If you run out of space above, no problem! We have extra "Ultimate Action Plans" for you in the back of the guide.

Well, now that you've created your Ultimate Action Plan, that's a wrap! I am thrilled for you as you begin your exciting college journey. With this information in hand, you're well on your way to finding your path in life and becoming the successful individual you were born to be! I wish you all the best.

appendix

. . . .

ncluded in these pages are extra action plan sheets, for you to flesh out your goals, plans, and strategies for success in greater detail. Several "My Notes" sheets are also included, for journaling, taking extra notes, doodling, or whatever purpose you choose!

ACTION PLAN: Class Act

First semester
Goal 1: _____

_____

Sub-goal 1: _____

_____

Date for completion: _____

_____

My reward for achieving the goal: _____

_____

Sub-goal 2: _____

_____

Date for completion: _____

_____

My reward for achieving the goal: _____

_____

Sub-goal 3: _____

_____

Date for completion: _____

_____

My reward for achieving the goal: _____

_____

Goal 2: _____

_____

Sub-goal 1: _____

_____

Date for completion: _____

_____

My reward for achieving the goal: _____

_____

Sub-goal 2: _____

_____

Date for completion: _____

_____

My reward for achieving the goal: _____

_____

Sub-goal 3: _____

_____

Date for completion: _____

_____

My reward for achieving the goal: _____

_____

Goal 3: _____

_____

Sub-goal 1: _____

_____

Date for completion: _____

_____

My reward for achieving the goal: _____

_____

Sub-goal 2: _____

_____

Date for completion: _____

_____

My reward for achieving the goal: _____

_____

Sub-goal 3: _____

_____

Date for completion: _____

_____

My reward for achieving the goal: _____

_____

Second semester
Goal 1: _____

_____

Sub-goal 1: _____

_____

Date for completion: _____

_____

My reward for achieving the goal: _____

_____

Sub-goal 2: _____

_____

Date for completion: _____

_____

My reward for achieving the goal: _____

_____

Sub-goal 3: _____

_____

Date for completion: _____

_____

My reward for achieving the goal: _____

_____

Goal 2: _____

_____

Sub-goal 1: _____

_____

Date for completion: _____

_____

My reward for achieving the goal: _____

_____

Sub-goal 2: _____

_____

Date for completion: _____

_____

My reward for achieving the goal: _____

_____

Sub-goal 3: _____

_____

Date for completion: _____

_____

My reward for achieving the goal: _____

_____

Goal 3: _____

_____

Sub-goal 1: _____

_____

Date for completion: _____

_____

My reward for achieving the goal: _____

_____

Sub-goal 2: _____

_____

Date for completion: _____

_____

My reward for achieving the goal: _____

_____

Sub-goal 3: _____

_____

Date for completion: _____

_____

My reward for achieving the goal: _____

_____

Goals I want to accomplish before graduation
Goal 1: _____

_____

Sub-goal 1: _____

_____

Date for completion: _____

_____

My reward for achieving the goal: _____

_____

Sub-goal 2: _____

_____

Date for completion: _____

_____

My reward for achieving the goal: _____

_____

Sub-goal 3: _____

_____

Date for completion: _____

_____

My reward for achieving the goal: _____

_____

Goal 2: _____

_____

Sub-goal 1: _____

_____

Date for completion: _____

_____

My reward for achieving the goal: _____

_____

Sub-goal 2: _____

_____

Date for completion: _____

_____

My reward for achieving the goal: _____

_____

Sub-goal 3: _____

_____

Date for completion: _____

_____

My reward for achieving the goal: _____

_____

Goal 3: _____

_____

Sub-goal 1: _____

_____

Date for completion: _____

_____

My reward for achieving the goal: _____

_____

Sub-goal 2: _____

Date for completion: _____

_____

My reward for achieving the goal: _____

_____

Sub-goal 3: _____

Date for completion: _____

_____

My reward for achieving the goal: _____

_____

ACTION PLAN: Class Act

First semester
Goal 1: _____

_____

Sub-goal 1: _____

_____

Date for completion: _____

_____

My reward for achieving the goal: _____

_____

Sub-goal 2: _____

_____

Date for completion: _____

_____

My reward for achieving the goal: _____

_____

Sub-goal 3: _____

_____

Date for completion: _____

_____

My reward for achieving the goal: _____

_____

Goal 2: _____

_____

Sub-goal 1: _____

_____

Date for completion: _____

_____

My reward for achieving the goal: _____

_____

Sub-goal 2: _____

_____

Date for completion: _____

_____

My reward for achieving the goal: _____

_____

Sub-goal 3: _____

_____

Date for completion: _____

_____

My reward for achieving the goal: _____

_____

Goal 3: _____

_____

Sub-goal 1: _____

_____

Date for completion: _____

_____

My reward for achieving the goal: _____

_____

Sub-goal 2: _____

_____

Date for completion: _____

_____

My reward for achieving the goal: _____

_____

Sub-goal 3: _____

_____

Date for completion: _____

_____

My reward for achieving the goal: _____

_____

Second semester
Goal 1: _____

_____

Sub-goal 1: _____

_____

Date for completion: _____

_____

My reward for achieving the goal: _____

_____

Sub-goal 2: _____

_____

Date for completion: _____

_____

My reward for achieving the goal: _____

_____

Sub-goal 3: _____

_____

Date for completion: _____

_____

My reward for achieving the goal: _____

_____

Goal 2: _____

_____

Sub-goal 1: _____

_____

Date for completion: _____

_____

My reward for achieving the goal: _____

_____

Sub-goal 2: _____

_____

Date for completion: _____

_____

My reward for achieving the goal: _____

_____

Sub-goal 3: _____

_____

Date for completion: _____

_____

My reward for achieving the goal: _____

_____

Goal 3: _____

_____

Sub-goal 1: _____

_____

Date for completion: _____

_____

My reward for achieving the goal: _____

_____

Sub-goal 2: _____

_____

Date for completion: _____

_____

My reward for achieving the goal: _____

_____

Sub-goal 3: _____

_____

Date for completion: _____

_____

My reward for achieving the goal: _____

_____

Goals I want to accomplish before graduation
Goal 1: _____

_____

Sub-goal 1: _____

_____

Date for completion: _____

_____

My reward for achieving the goal: _____

_____

Sub-goal 2: _____

_____

Date for completion: _____

_____

My reward for achieving the goal: _____

_____

Sub-goal 3: _____

_____

Date for completion: _____

_____

My reward for achieving the goal: _____

_____

Goal 2: _____

_____

Sub-goal 1: _____

_____

Date for completion: _____

_____

My reward for achieving the goal: _____

_____

Sub-goal 2: _____

_____

Date for completion: _____

_____

My reward for achieving the goal: _____

_____

Sub-goal 3: _____

_____

Date for completion: _____

_____

My reward for achieving the goal: _____

_____

Goal 3: _____

_____

Sub-goal 1: _____

_____

Date for completion: _____

_____

My reward for achieving the goal: _____

_____

Sub-goal 2: _____

_____

Date for completion: _____

_____

My reward for achieving the goal: _____

_____

Sub-goal 3: _____

_____

Date for completion: _____

_____

My reward for achieving the goal: _____

_____

ACTION PLAN: *Campus & Community Maven*

To create your action plan for outside of class, start by choosing your top three goals in life. Don't stress too much about what they are right now. Just follow what your heart tells you. Reference the list of activities on campus and in the community, and then pick the ones that seem to be most related to your goals, along with the level of involvement that you'll need to commit to making them happen.

I've filled out a sample one to help get you started:

Sample goal: Running for public office

Possible activities: Student government; volunteering for local nonprofit; local school board

Level of involvement: Run for a leadership position for any of these organizations

Goal 1: _____

_____

Possible activities: _____

_____

_____

_____

Level of involvement: _____

_____

_____

_____

Goal 2: _____

_____

Possible activities: _____

_____

_____

_____

Level of involvement: _____

_____

_____

_____

Goal 3: _____

_____

Possible activities: _____

_____

_____

_____

Level of involvement: _____

_____

_____

_____

ACTION PLAN: Campus & Community Maven

To create your action plan for outside of class, start by choosing your top three goals in life. Don't stress too much about what they are right now. Just follow what your heart tells you. Reference the list of activities on campus and in the community, and then pick the ones that seem to be most related to your goals, along with the level of involvement that you'll need to commit to making them happen.

I've filled out a sample one to help get you started:

Sample goal: Running for public office

Possible activities: Student government; volunteering for local nonprofit; local school board

Level of involvement: Run for a leadership position for any of these organizations

Goal 1: _____

_____

Possible activities: _____

_____

_____

_____

Level of involvement: _____

_____

_____

_____

Goal 2: _____

_____

Possible activities: _____

_____

_____

_____

Level of involvement: _____

_____

_____

_____

Goal 3: _____

_____

Possible activities: _____

_____

_____

_____

Level of involvement: _____

_____

_____

_____

ACTION PLAN: Sorority Life

Now you have an idea what to expect when rushing and know the lingo for the process. Ready to move forward in exploring sorority membership? It's now time for you to create a plan of action.

As we previously discussed, meeting potential sorority sisters is a lot like interviewing, so it's important to have something to offer to the conversation that shows that you're invested in the success of the sorority itself. Here's a simple step-by-step process for getting ready to rush.

STEP 1: Familiarize yourself with the sororities on campus and what makes them tick.

Having this knowledge in your back pocket will not only impress your potential future sisters, it will also give you something to fall back on if you run out of things to say.

What were some of their recent events on campus? What was the impact?

What charity fund-raisers did they hold?

Were there any great accomplishments by certain members? (i.e., Was a member selected as a top Greek member on campus?)

Did the chapter receive campus or national awards for its efforts?

STEP 2: Think about ways your background and experience can aid each sorority in its future success.

One way to help you stand out from the crowd of other PNMs is to offer up ideas on how *you* can make a difference within each chapter. This is great practice for when you have a *real* job interview, plus it helps you to better define the special characteristics and traits that make you a stand-out. Come up with a list of five skills or qualifications you can use to differentiate yourself from your fellow rush participants. Here's a list of questions to get you thinking:

Are you an amazing planner?

A whiz with technology?

Do you get really good grades, and are you open to tutoring other sisters?

Do you have a talent for singing or stage performance that could come in handy for the annual spring talent revue?

STEP 3: Create a list of talking points.

Every college freshman who's taken Psych 101 knows that we're all drawn to the familiar. In laymen's terms, this means we subconsciously want to be around people and places that are in sync with our own likes and beliefs. This is why talking points unrelated to sorority life can be extremely helpful.

Obsessed with *Twilight*? Love to bargain shop? Concerned about the environmental impact the oil spill in the Gulf Coast will have on wildlife ten years down the road? Write up a list of five to ten topics that you can use as conversation starters. These subjects are *exactly* what you will need to gain inroads with potential sorority sisters and new friends you might meet along the way during the rush process.

List them here:

1. _____

    _____

    _____

2. _____

    _____

    _____

3. _____

    _____

    _____

4. _____

    _____

    _____

5. _____

    _____

    _____

6. _____

_____

_____

7. _____

_____

_____

8. _____

_____

_____

9. _____

_____

_____

10. _____

_____

_____

ACTION PLAN: Sorority Life

Now you have an idea what to expect when rushing and know the lingo for the process. Ready to move forward in exploring sorority membership? It's now time for you to create a plan of action.

As we previously discussed, meeting potential sorority sisters is a lot like interviewing, so it's important to have something to offer to the conversation that shows that you're invested in the success of the sorority itself. Here's a simple step-by-step process for getting ready to rush.

STEP 1: Familiarize yourself with the sororities on campus and what makes them tick.

Having this knowledge in your back pocket will not only impress your potential future sisters, it will also give you something to fall back on if you run out of things to say.

What were some of their recent events on campus? What was the impact?

What charity fund-raisers did they hold?

Were there any great accomplishments by certain members? (i.e., Was a member selected as a top Greek member on campus?)

Did the chapter receive campus or national awards for its efforts?

STEP 2: Think about ways your background and experience can aid each sorority in its future success.

One way to help you stand out from the crowd of other PNMs is to offer up ideas on how *you* can make a difference within each chapter. This is great practice for when you have a *real* job interview, plus it helps you to better define the special characteristics and traits that make you a stand-out. Come up with a list of five skills or qualifications you can use to differentiate yourself from your fellow rush participants. Here's a list of questions to get you thinking:

Are you an amazing planner?

A whiz with technology?

Do you get really good grades, and are you open to tutoring other sisters?

Do you have a talent for singing or stage performance that could come in handy for the annual spring talent revue?

STEP 3: Create a list of talking points.

Every college freshman who's taken Psych 101 knows that we're all drawn to the familiar. In laymen's terms, this means we subconsciously want to be around people and places that are in sync with our own likes and beliefs. This is why talking points unrelated to sorority life can be extremely helpful.

Obsessed with *Twilight*? Love to bargain shop? Concerned about the environmental impact the oil spill in the Gulf Coast will have on wildlife ten years down the road? Write up a list of five to ten topics that you can use as conversation starters. These subjects are *exactly* what you will need to gain inroads with potential sorority sisters and new friends you might meet along the way during the rush process.

List them here:

1. _____
   _____
   _____

2. _____
   _____
   _____

3. _____
   _____
   _____

4. _____
   _____
   _____

5. _____
   _____
   _____

6. _____

_____

_____

7. _____

_____

_____

8. _____

_____

_____

9. _____

_____

_____

10. _____

_____

_____

ACTION PLAN: Relationships

What are some new ways you can try to conquer that homesickness? We've filled out an example to get you started:

Goal: <u>End homesickness</u>

1. New Activity: <u>Sign up for intramural basketball.</u>
   How Often: <u>Practice twice per week.</u>

2. New Activity: <u>Audition for the school choir.</u>
   How Often: <u>Practice once per week.</u>

3. New Activity: <u>Go through informal sorority recruitment.</u>
   How Often: <u>Can start as soon as I contact the Panhellenic Council office on campus.</u>

Now it's your turn. Try to come up with at least three new social activities to try:

Goal: _____

1. New Activity: _____
   How Often: _____

2. New Activity: _____
   How Often: _____

3. New Activity: _____
   How Often: _____

4. New Activity: _____
   How Often: _____

5. New Activity: _____
   How Often: _____

6. New Activity: _____
   How Often: _____

ACTION PLAN: Relationships

What are some new ways you can try to conquer that homesickness? We've filled out an example to get you started:

Goal: End homesickness

1. New Activity: Sign up for intramural basketball.
   How Often: Practice twice per week.

2. New Activity: Audition for the school choir.
   How Often: Practice once per week.

3. New Activity: Go through informal sorority recruitment.
   How Often: Can start as soon as I contact the Panhellenic Council office on campus.

Now it's your turn. Try to come up with at least three new social activities to try:

Goal: _____

1. New Activity: _____
   How Often: _____

2. New Activity: _____
   How Often: _____

3. New Activity: _____
   How Often: _____

4. New Activity: _____
   How Often: _____

5. New Activity: _____
   How Often: _____

6. New Activity: _____
   How Often: _____

ACTION PLAN: Build My Network

Career goal: Become a lawyer at a nongovernmental organization.

Potential people to meet: Find an alum who works in the legal field and request a phone call.

How? Contact alumni relations department to see if they have an alumni network; attend three pre-law networking events on campus.

Now it's your turn to complete the action plan.

Career goal: _____

_____

_____

Potential people to meet: _____

_____

_____

How? _____

_____

_____

Career goal: _____

_____

_____

Potential people to meet: _____

_____

_____

How? _____

_____

_____

ACTION PLAN: Build My Network

Career goal: <u>Become a lawyer at a nongovernmental organization.</u>

Potential people to meet: <u>Find an alum who works in the legal field and request a phone call.</u>

How? <u>Contact alumni relations department to see if they have an alumni network; attend three pre-law networking events on campus.</u>

Now it's your turn to complete the action plan.

Career goal: _____

_____

_____

Potential people to meet: _____

_____

_____

How? _____

_____

_____

Career goal: _____

_____

_____

Potential people to meet: _____

_____

How? _____

_____

_____

ACTION PLAN: Healthy Me

List three fitness goals for your first year of college, and try be as specific as possible (i.e., run in a race—5K, 10K, or even further; complete a season on an intramural team; improve strength/endurance; etc.):

1. _____

   _____

2. _____

   _____

3. _____

   _____

List at least three forms of exercise you enjoy or would like to try that will help you reach the goals you've listed above (i.e., running, biking, swimming, strength training, kickboxing, intramural team sports, etc.):

1. _____

   _____

2. _____

   _____

3. _____

   _____

List as many things you can think of that will help you meet these goals (i.e., find a workout partner, get good running shoes, schedule workouts into your day, etc.):

_____

_____

_____

_____

_____

Finally, plan out a weekly schedule for the semester that incorporates the fitness goals you listed:

Day	Activity	Length of time	Things that will help me meet this goal
Monday			
Tuesday			
Wednesday			
Thursday			
Friday			
Saturday			
Sunday			

ACTION PLAN: Healthy Me

List three fitness goals for your first year of college, and try be as specific as possible (i.e., run in a race—5K, 10K, or even further; complete a season on an intramural team; improve strength/endurance; etc.):

1. _____

_____

2. _____

_____

3. _____

_____

List at least three forms of exercise you enjoy or would like to try that will help you reach the goals you've listed above (i.e., running, biking, swimming, strength training, kickboxing, intramural team sports, etc.):

1. _____

_____

2. _____

_____

3. _____

_____

List as many things you can think of that will help you meet these goals (i.e., find a workout partner, get good running shoes, schedule workouts into your day, etc.):

_____

_____

_____

_____

_____

Finally, plan out a weekly schedule for the semester that incorporates the fitness goals you listed:

Day	Activity	Length of time	Things that will help me meet this goal
Monday			
Tuesday			
Wednesday			
Thursday			
Friday			
Saturday			
Sunday			

ACTION PLAN: The College Budget
SEMESTER BUDGET WORKSHEET FOR COLLEGE STUDENTS

CATEGORY	SEMESTER BUDGET	SEMESTER ACTUAL	SEMESTER DIFFERENCE
INCOME:			
From Jobs			
From Parents			
From Student Loans			
From Scholarships			
From Other Financial Aid			
Miscellaneous Income			
INCOME SUBTOTAL			
EXPENSES:			
Rent or Room & Board			
Utilities			
Telephone			
Groceries			
Toiletries/Makeup			
Car Payment/Transportation			
Insurance			
Gasoline/Oil			
Repairs and Maintenance			
Entertainment			
Eating Out/Vending			
Tuition			
Books			
School Fees			
Computer Expenses			
Miscellaneous Expenses			
EXPENSES SUBTOTAL			
NET INCOME (INCOME LESS EXPENSES)			

If an expense is incurred more or less often than once each semester, convert it to a semester amount when filling out the budget. For instance, an auto expense that is billed every year would be converted to a semester by dividing the amount in half.

It's also important to point out that, when totaling your net income, the goal is to not end up in the hole or with a negative number. If you did, go back and adjust your budget amounts, so you come out on top.

ACTION PLAN: The College Budget

SEMESTER BUDGET WORKSHEET FOR COLLEGE STUDENTS

CATEGORY	SEMESTER BUDGET	SEMESTER ACTUAL	SEMESTER DIFFERENCE
INCOME:			
From Jobs			
From Parents			
From Student Loans			
From Scholarships			
From Other Financial Aid			
Miscellaneous Income			
INCOME SUBTOTAL			
EXPENSES:			
Rent or Room & Board			
Utilities			
Telephone			
Groceries			
Toiletries/Makeup			
Car Payment/Transportation			
Insurance			
Gasoline/Oil			
Repairs and Maintenance			
Entertainment			
Eating Out/Vending			
Tuition			
Books			
School Fees			
Computer Expenses			
Miscellaneous Expenses			
EXPENSES SUBTOTAL			
NET INCOME (INCOME LESS EXPENSES)			

If an expense is incurred more or less often than once each semester, convert it to a semester amount when filling out the budget. For instance, an auto expense that is billed every year would be converted to a semester by dividing the amount in half.

It's also important to point out that, when totaling your net income, the goal is to not end up in the hole or with a negative number. If you did, go back and adjust your budget amounts, so you come out on top.

ACTION PLAN: Career Queen

PHASE 1:

❏ Talk with your academic advisor and a career services counselor to find out what internship resources are available to you on campus.

Deadline: _____

❏ Write your resume and cover letter.

Deadline: _____

❏ Decide what you would like from your internship. Responsibilities? Compensation? Experience?

Deadline: _____

❏ Attend job fairs to find opportunities.

Deadline: _____

❏ Attend networking events and reach out to anyone who might know of an opportunity.

Deadline: _____

❏ Define where you would like to do your internship. City? Corporation? Industry?

Deadline: _____

❏ Start researching possibilities. Obtain general information about the company, internship programs, contact people, and deadlines.

Deadline: _____

PHASE 2:

❏ Send out your resume and cover letter.

Deadline: _____

❏ Practice your interviewing skills. Schedule a mock interview with your career services office.

Deadline: _____

PHASE 3:

❏ Make sure your application is complete for each company where you would like to intern.

Deadline: _____

❏ Interview with employers.

Deadline: _____

❏ Send thank-you letters to employers who gave you an opportunity to interview.

Deadline: _____

ACTION PLAN: Career Queen

PHASE 1:

❏ Talk with your academic advisor and a career services counselor to find out what internship resources are available to you on campus.

Deadline: _____

❏ Write your resume and cover letter.

Deadline: _____

❏ Decide what you would like from your internship. Responsibilities? Compensation? Experience?

Deadline: _____

❏ Attend job fairs to find opportunities.

Deadline: _____

❏ Attend networking events and reach out to anyone who might know of an opportunity.

Deadline: _____

❏ Define where you would like to do your internship. City? Corporation? Industry?

Deadline: _____

❏ Start researching possibilities. Obtain general information about the company, internship programs, contact people, and deadlines.

Deadline: _____

PHASE 2:

❏ Send out your resume and cover letter.

Deadline: _____

❏ Practice your interviewing skills. Schedule a mock interview with your career services office.

Deadline: _____

PHASE 3:

❏ Make sure your application is complete for each company where you would like to intern.

Deadline: _____

❏ Interview with employers.

Deadline: _____

❏ Send thank-you letters to employers who gave you an opportunity to interview.

Deadline: _____

The Ultimate Action Plan

KEY AREAS	WHAT DO I WANT TO ACHIEVE?	HOW AM I GOING TO ACHIEVE IT?	TARGET DATE FOR COMPLETION?
Defining Who You Are			
Class Act			
Campus & Community Maven			
Sorority Life			
Relationships			

KEY AREAS	WHAT DO I WANT TO ACHIEVE?	HOW AM I GOING TO ACHIEVE IT?	TARGET DATE FOR COMPLETION?
Build My Network			
Healthy Me			
The College Budget			
Career Queen			

The Ultimate Action Plan

KEY AREAS	WHAT DO I WANT TO ACHIEVE?	HOW AM I GOING TO ACHIEVE IT?	TARGET DATE FOR COMPLETION?
Defining Who You Are			
Class Act			
Campus & Community Maven			
Sorority Life			
Relationships			

KEY AREAS	WHAT DO I WANT TO ACHIEVE?	HOW AM I GOING TO ACHIEVE IT?	TARGET DATE FOR COMPLETION?
Build My Network			
Healthy Me			
The College Budget			
Career Queen			

My Notes

My Notes

My Notes

My Notes

My Notes

My Notes

My Notes

My Notes

about christie garton

· ·

Christie Garton is the leading expert on the college experience for women. She is an award-winning social entrepreneur; founder of UniversityChic .com, an online magazine and community website for college women nationwide; and author of *U Chic: The College Girl's Guide to Everything*, a bestselling guide for college women. She has served as college life expert for Seventeen.com and *Wall Street Journal*, and has contributed to *U.S.News & World Report* and *USA TODAY*.

© Steve Attig

A graduate of the University of Kansas and the University of Pennsylvania Law School, Christie also serves as a judge for the annual USA TODAY Academic All-Star competition, helping select the "best and brightest" college students each year.

about u chic

· · · · · · · · · · · · · · · · · · ·

The U Chic book series and product line was created by Christie Garton, founder of www.UniversityChic.com—the #1 online resource for college women—to help young women succeed in school and life.

U Chic: The College Girl's Guide to Everything

A fully updated guide for women to the entire college experience, from the day the acceptance letter arrives to graduation.

978-1-4022-5495-6
$14.99 U.S./£9.99 UK

U Chic College Planner

A student planner to help you get organized and keep track of your fabulous college life.

$12.99 U.S./£9.99 UK

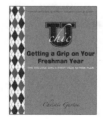

U Chic's Getting a Grip on Your Freshman Year: The College Girl's First Year Action Plan

A companion workbook focused on helping you take action during your freshman year to have a successful college transition.

978-1-4022-4398-1
$16.99 U.S./£11.99 UK

U Chic College Scrapbook

A fashionable scrapbook perfect for preserving college memories forever.

978-1-4022-4400-1
$22.99 U.S.